ERIC FRANKLIN

# PEANUT BUTTER

# PRINCIPLES

## 47 Leadership Lessons
### Every Parent Should Teach Their Kids

# Peanut Butter Principles
*47 Leadership Lessons Every Parent Should Teach Their Kids*

Copyright © 2013 by Eric Franklin

**Everilis Books**
P.O. Box 1077
Dunkirk, MD 20754
info@everilis.com

ISBN-10: 0615912826
ISBN-13: 978-0-615-91282-0

Book Design by Sherwin Soy
Editing by Sue Publicover

**Ordering Information:**Quantity sales. Special discounts are available on quantity purchases by corporations, associations, schools and others. For details, contact the publisher at the address above.

The author may be available for live events within the continental U.S. He speaks on entrepreneurship, business coaching and development, personal productivity, maintaining values while achieving success, and youth character development. Inquire at info@peanutbutterprinciples.com

Printed in the United States of America

**Disclaimer:** This publication is designed to provide accurate and personal experience information in regard to the subject matter covered. It is sold with the understanding that the author, contributors, publisher are not engaged in rendering counseling or other professional services. If counseling advice or other expert assistance is required, the services of a competent professional person should be sought out.

# ACKNOWLEDGEMENTS

To my children—Evan, Erica, and Elisa—for whom I wrote this book as a love letter and instruction manual for life.

To Rané, my spouse and partner in the raising of our children and who is esteemed in her own right as a staunch advocate for children and youth.

To my parents and grandparents, who unknowingly, deposited in me a lifetime of *Peanut Butter Principles*, many of which are contained within these pages.

*Even though this is not a "religion" book, it is unapologetically, based on a lifelong faith that was instilled into me from birth by my parents. As an adult, I am encouraged by three men who have enriched my life through their dedication to their calling:*

To John A. Cherry, who connected the dots for me to grow through the uncompromising life lessons I needed in my early adulthood, and who gave me the opportunity to serve in leadership capacities that shaped my management outlook to this day,

To John K. Jenkins, my pastor, a regular guy who is continually used by God to encourage everyday people in extraordinary ways.

To Leonard N. Smith, whose perspective keeps me constantly challenged and growing.

To all the young people in my family, community and across the world who choose to seriously consider the wisdom of these words.

# CONTENTS

# PREFACE

Probably my dad's favorite possession is a set of dusty cassette tapes with recordings of his dad speaking on the front porch of his home 35 years ago. They represent, perhaps, the final and lasting testimony in his own words by a man who lived a simple life, but who was well respected and loved throughout his family and community. The conversation was in no way remarkable or profound, just a conversation about a life well lived.

I have built my life's work in pursuit of finding a better way. I am a management consultant by trade and an entrepreneur at heart. I have been very successful building businesses and people to be the best they can be. Some say that I'm a pretty good business coach; I'd like to think that I'm good at nurturing the gifts of individuals to the benefit of their businesses and employers. As a public speaker, I am often asked to speak on how to start ventures or how to move them to the next level, "*Getting Past Go*". I was in the midst of writing a *Getting Past Go* book, and I felt the inspiration to put that book aside and concentrate on something else. Because my wife and I waited longer than most to have children, I wanted to make sure that my children and others who look to me for guidance were not left without the tools to succeed. This is my legacy.

As many people do, after my career seemed to be progressing on auto-pilot, I began to volunteer a lot of time to organizations that help people overcome environmental, educational, economic, and social challenges. I've hired hundreds, possibly thousands of people during my career and as a naturally inquisitive and analytical person, I began to ponder why some people are successful and others aren't. I concluded that it goes back to foundation.

I was fortunate to be raised in a solidly middle-class neighborhood in Richmond, Virginia. We had doctors and lawyers, laborers and secretaries, teachers and factory workers, all co-existing in one ecology—which is not to suggest that all the kids didn't know the economic status of those who were better- or worse-off than the average. We knew—and most people assumed that over time, the most "successful" adults would produce the most successful children. That was not the case.

What I noticed was that the common denominator in determining whether a person of this neighborhood would excel in life was whether or not they were raised under a firm set of principles—not rules, but principles that were easy to comprehend, remember, and apply to a lifetime of situations.

*Peanut Butter Principles* is my attempt to share with all who will listen, guideposts to help parents develop their kids into the leaders of today and tomorrow.

*"It is easier to build strong children than to repair broken men."*
—Frederick Douglass

· · · · · · · · · · · · · · · · · · · · · · · · · · · · · · · · · · · · · · · · · · · · · · · · · · · · · · ·

· ·

# INTRODUCTION

Life is a trip.

It's a winding road of turns, stops, and detours. And if it's true that "you learn something new every day", then we are all walking encyclopedias of knowledge, insight, and experience. No two people are the same, because their unique journeys have provided them with different viewpoints.

I often marvel at the amount of information we gather up in our lives. Some of it may seem useless—unless you're competing on "Jeopardy"— but you never know when a tidbit in your recollection will surface at just the right moment.

As a parent, I find myself filtering through the life lessons I've learned— some better than others—over the fifty-plus years I've been blessed with so far. I've had my share of eye-opening epiphanies and stirring wake-up calls. I've made both good choices and bad. And when I see my kids facing decisions, I do my best to impart the wisdom that can only come with age, and then hope they are paying attention.

I'm not talking about the things like "don't touch the stove—it's hot" and "don't talk to strangers", because those are givens (or should be). We naturally try to shield our children from physical pain and injury. We also do our best to help them heal from life's disappointments, like the day someone finally keeps score on the playing field or when not every kid in the group receives an award. We try to protect them from the cruelty of bullying, which has become a mightier task than our own parents had to deal with in the pre-Internet age, before the taunts and torment shifted to 24/7.

Aside from protecting my children, I am trying to empower them with the knowledge and skills that will benefit them when I'm not around—in those moments when my son or daughter is too proud or too worried about repercussions to seek my help.

We've all had to make tough choices throughout our lives. Sometimes, we chose correctly, but not always. For me, I have tried to learn from those decisions and outcomes, no matter what side of the good-bad scale I was perched.

In those rare, quiet moments of parental reflection, I began making a list of the life lessons I wanted to share with my children. The power of the written word somehow makes thoughts more real, just as deliberate action turns a wish into a tangible goal. Hmmmm…there's another one to add to the growing list.

As I remembered experiences in my past, lessons learned from mentors (including my parents and grandparents), I added them to this list. Sometimes, we would all be seated around the dinner table, and my wife or one of the kids would mention something that they saw, heard, or did, and it would trigger another item for my list. Or a church sermon would spark a worthy thought. Or a conversation with a colleague at work would cause me to pull out my smartphone and tap in an entry for the ever-growing life lessons list.

At first, it was just my intention to go through this list with my family. But once it grew to more than 35 items, I felt like I had something more to share, and that it might have value to other parents and mentors as well.

The children we are raising today face a much broader spectrum of challenges and opportunities than we ever had. Technology has changed the way they communicate, and with whom. We no longer worry only about the stranger near the bus stop, but the ones lurking in the shadows of the World Wide Web. That wonderful smartphone that lets us stay connected with our kids is also a tool that could lead to anything from heartache to felonies. And bullying isn't limited to the playground any more. It's permeating every corner of a child's life.

It has become so much harder to protect our kids. As parents, we now need to focus substantial energy on empowering them with the tools to make good decisions when we're not there to help them. We need to give them the confidence, esteem, awareness, empathy, and control to thrive—not just survive—in the world. We have to help them learn to not just see opportunities, but create them.

As I reflect on the lessons I need to impart to my children so that they are empowered to be the best they can be, I realize that many of the principles I live by are, in fact, very simple and basic. Situations and predicaments often can be very complicated, however, usually the answer to the problem emanates out of some fundamental and foundational principles.

Many children are "picky" eaters. They may like something one week and detest it the next. According to my wife, one of our daughters will not eat pears or bananas; however, I've never had a problem getting her to eat the fruit (I guess daddy has that special touch). She probably gets it from me. I think I vaguely remember putting my parents through a similar ordeal with milk and beans and pickles and oysters and… well, the list was long. I always knew that, if my mom served any number of menu items I deplored, after I sheepishly consumed the *required minimum* serving, I would still be hungry. There was always something I liked in the pantry—peanut butter, and a peanut butter and jelly sandwich was the first "meal" my parents allowed me to make on my own. To this day, if I can't find something I want that's fast and satisfying and something that'll "hold me over" to the next meal, you might find me reaching for that jar of peanut butter.

And then it hit me. Peanut Butter Principles. Those lessons that should stick to a kid with the same clinginess as a gooey mouthful of peanut butter. Spoon feed them the wisdom you want them to have, one bite at a time. And do it with flavor.

Although I talk about "parents" here, I have to mention that more and more grandparents are playing an integral role in the lives of children. Many are responsible for raising their grandchildren, in place of the parents, and others are living in multi-generational homes. Don't underestimate "the wisdom of the ages" as it is a timeless bridge across the generations.

I want my children to mature into good, balanced, and happy adults. I hope they will develop the leadership skills that will drive them to succeed in every aspect of their lives—personal and professional, emotional and intellectual. And I hope that someday they will make their own additions to this list and share these valuable lessons with their own children.

I've worked hard to provide for my family, but I know that financial security is only one element of my role as a parent. The lessons I am including in this book represent my commitment to nurturing young people into good citizens, strong leaders, and happy, fulfilled individuals.

## How this book "works"

The book is divided into five sections:

1. **The Super Self**—building the internal skill set of self-confidence, self-awareness, self-esteem, and self-control

2. **Making Wishes Come True**—understanding the importance of

setting and achieving goals

3. **The School of Life**—fundamental wisdom that will smooth out the bumpy journey

4. **Relationships**—learning how to interact with others in a positive way

5. **Good Choices**—gaining the ability to improve decision-making

While there is no hard-and-fast schedule for the lessons here, I've designed the book to follow a logical (at least in my perspective) order. You have to start somewhere, so I suggest you begin at the beginning and help your child build character with the lessons in the first section. In this way, you have a youth who is better prepared to move on to goal-setting in the second section. With more self-awareness, a child can identify worthy goals and, with self-control, can set about achieving them. Building strong character enables a child to handle challenges, deal with people, and make tough choices—like standing up to peers and doing the right thing instead of the easy one.

You also need to recognize that you can't flood a child's mind with all this insight at once. It's not a race. Work through the items one at a time until you're sure the child has a good grasp on the lesson and is ready to move on to the next one. If you make this a weekly experience, for example, you could complete the book in a year's time.

**❝** *You also need to recognize that you can't flood a child's mind with all this insight at once. It's not a race.*❞

Also be aware that the ideas in this book are not just geared toward kids. We all have room to grow and you can become a great role model for the people in your life when you show that you yourself are open to making positive changes.

After that, my advice is to keep going. Start again from the beginning. Education and growth have no end if you move through life with both your eyes and your mind wide open.

One final thought before we press on: I don't profess to have compiled all the answers to life's mysteries here in this book. I am only sharing the nuggets that I have unearthed. It's a start. Add or subtract, as you see fit. And please share your thoughts and ideas with me. This list should keep growing so that we create a volume that our kids can pass along to their own. The challenges will continue to change and mount, but with the guidance from those of us who have "been there, done that", we are giving youth the chance to flourish.

PART

# THE SUPER SELF

Let's start at the beginning. What makes a good person? A strong leader? An individual who leads a happy, healthy, fulfilled life?

There are basic skills and traits that we need to sharpen in ourselves and the best time to do this is in the early part of life's journey. "The Super Self" is the keen awareness of who you want to be and making the concerted effort to become that person. It's the ability to recognize and live by values that matter, whether or not anyone is looking.

When we can raise kids to love and respect themselves, first and foremost, then we take giant steps toward a brighter future for everyone.

# 1 | "Life is not fair. Get over it."

Do you remember your first major disappointment? Maybe Santa didn't bring the toy you had been aching for or you didn't win a race or contest. Or possibly it was the first time you felt the pain of unrequited love. Disappointment comes from expectations that aren't met.

It happens. That's what we call "the real world". Life is fraught with disappointments, heartbreak, and rejection. Sure, it feels unfair sometimes, but there's no rulebook for life that says the playing field will always be level. We are given chances and choices all along this journey. And even when you feel you've made the right decisions and played your best, sometimes, you still don't win.

**❝ ...*there's no rulebook for life that says the playing field will always be level.*"**

In order to truly appreciate what we have, we need to experience the unfair things in life. Shielding children from loss and rejection gives them an unrealistic sense of accomplishment. When every child walks away from a competition with a ribbon or a medal, these prizes reward them just for the act of showing up; it has nothing to do with excellence. Years later, do you think a college professor will applaud every student who shows up to class or an employer will pat each employee on the back for arriving on time to work? Of course not. But these are the behaviors for which children are rewarded. So, they come to expect accolades for what should simply be expected of them.

Children can only become exceptional when they have a realistic view of what this measure really is. When we do everything possible to level the playing field, how can they possibly rise above the status quo? How can they differentiate between mediocre, average, and excellent? A person who sees the world as unfair is probably looking at it from the bottom rung of the ladder—not a leader, but someone who blames the world for what he hasn't had the ability to overcome.

> **❝ *A person who sees the world as unfair is probably looking at it from the bottom rung of the ladder...* ❞**

Now, consider the tee ball games where no one keeps score so as not to differentiate between a winning team and a losing one, which creates a crew of sad youngsters. In these games, each child gets many more chances to swing at the ball than they would if the game were played according to the rules. But, hey, they're just kids, so the parents all smile and pretend not to care, even though each one is making mental notes of their own kid's performance.

At what age is it appropriate to keep score? Four? Six? Ten? When is it okay for a child to learn the lesson of losing to someone else? If they have siblings and play games at home, they experience losing. And they probably lose to others on the playground. How do you then distinguish what's "fair"? By not keeping score in a game, is it fair to the person who is winning? By abolishing a student awards program—whether it's academic, athletic, musical, or otherwise—is it fair to the student who has made an extra effort to improve, just so that others won't feel less than stellar? Should colleges get rid of the Dean's List? Should the professionals cancel All-Star games?

Fairness weighs more heavily on the person who perceives himself to be on the losing end of any competition or choice. From the kid who is picked last for a team to the one who doesn't get invited to a birthday party, it all seems unfair. When your child works her hardest and still isn't chosen as Student of the Month or accepted into the college of her choice, you question the fairness of the decision. The parent whose child is warming the bench pressures the coach to put the kid in the game. While I agree that every player deserves a chance, it should be the coach's decision, not the parent's. And what happens when the child fails to live up to expectations, or, worse yet, makes an error that hurts the team? Then they all learn about losing, and you can't prevent that outcome.

If your daughter is tasked with selling Girl Scout cookies, is it fair to the other Scouts when you take the order sheet to your office, fitness club, hairdresser, dentist, and every other acquaintance in order to boost her sales? If your Cub Scout is preparing for the Pinewood Derby and you engineer a faster race car, will the boys who don't have a hands-on, handy helper to "pimp their rides" think your son's victory was earned fairly? And will the young student who made her own school project without adult intervention believe that another one who clearly had help deserves equal consideration for grades?

In the end, the parent's role is not to challenge those decision-makers or manipulate results. Instead, their job is to promote the development that sets the child up for success and then equip the child with the coping skills to handle the inevitable disappointments that will occur from time to time.

Adult intervention has created an entire generation of "helicopter parents" who swoop in to protect their kids from any type of harm. They hover over these children so much that the youngsters don't develop the ability to fly on their own—to make their own decisions, accept accountability for their actions, and handle disappointment, hurt, and rejection. What they *do* develop is an inflated sense of entitlement, believing the world owes them, not the other way around.

Generation Y—comprised of approximately 80 million people born between 1980 and 2001—has been raised with a sense of entitlement for instant gratification. The Internet gives them immediate access to information.

They download music in seconds, and carry it with them on mp3 players in their pockets—not clumsy Walkmans or boom boxes. They shop online—without the "hassle" of trekking from store to store, like we had to do—and with a couple of clicks, they get overnight delivery. They have microwaves so they don't have to wait for food. Their precious smartphones keep them in touch with their friends, wherever they are, whether via texting or social media. They have grown up with the expectation that everything they want is readily accessible. *Vini, vidi, accepi.* I came, I saw, I got.

Also known as "Millennials" and "Echo Boomers" (the children of Baby Boomers), this generation has been raised by parents who were committed to providing much more to their children than they had—even though technology has already given them an abundance of conveniences. In addition to financial security, Baby Boomer parents also strive to provide emotional security. Their efforts to demonstrate their love have stretched boundaries to the breaking point. Some helicopter parents have accompanied their young adults on college admission and job interviews, or intervened when a professor or employer wronged their child in some way.

In December 2012, college student Aubrey Ireland decided she had had enough of her parents' intervention. She was granted a civil stalking restraining order against her parents when their intrusions into her life became unbearable. Aubrey, an only child, says her mom was always "over-involved" in her life. When she went off to college, her mother insisted the young woman leave her computer on with her Skype account activated so the parents could watch her. They monitored her computer and her cell phone, and frequently drove 600 miles from their home in Kansas to the College-Conservatory of Music at the University of Cincinnati to drop in, unannounced, and check on their daughter.

The Conservatory hired security guards specifically to keep the parents out of the theater where Aubrey, a music theater major, was performing.

"I never wanted this to happen, that's the last thing I wanted," Aubrey said, "but I wasn't in control of my life at all anymore. I knew that they were holding me back emotionally, mentally, and professionally, and it got to the point where [the restraining order] was basically my last option."

The Irelands are an extreme case, but they represent how far helicopter parents will go in order to maintain control over their children's lives.

The sooner we relinquish that need to control and instead teach children that they will meet up with disappointment from time to time, the better, more well-rounded people they will become. They will have the emotional strength to weather tough times. They can handle rejection more effectively and channel their energy into more positive perspectives and endeavors. They will discover that they can learn from the losses, discovering more about themselves and making better decisions as a result. By learning from mistakes, they will be able to not only improve their own coping and decision-making skills, but they will also be able to more effectively guide others. They will use their experience as a useful growth tool, not a setback imposed unfairly on them.

A parent who doesn't pick up a child every time she cries is not being cruel, but rather showing that small person that certain behaviors aren't rewarded. If that child cries in a store to get what she wants, buying something just to "shut them up" communicates that bad behavior is the way to go. I doubt that any parent wants to reinforce that message.

An adult who offers advice for selling more cookies, making a better race car, or crafting a project worthy of a higher grade—rather than taking over the cause—teaches a child to take initiative, solve problems, and become independent. This is a young person who will know how to persevere in the face of challenge, not cave in under its weight.

Praise a child for making decisions. Don't bribe them. Teach them that the effort is as important as the outcome.

**"** *This is a young person who will know how to persevere in the face of challenge, not cave in under its weight."*

Remember the classic Rolling Stones lyrics:

>*"You can't always get what you want,*

>*But if you try sometime, you might just find*

>*You get what you need."*

Rather than fill children with a false sense of entitlement that will surely hold them back, let's teach youth that the world is filled with challenges. Frankly, I think that's what makes it interesting, and besides, the Bible states, "He makes his sun to rise on the evil and on the good, and sends rain on the just and on the unjust". Matt 5:45.

Get over it.

# 2 | "Love thyself."

I love watching little children learn. They grasp concepts so easily, unlike adults who make things so complicated that they hinder their own learning. That's why I have constantly struggled to learn Spanish as an adult while my children pick up languages seemingly at the drop of a hat.

Small children are like sponges. They absorb so much of what they see, hear, and experience—both good and bad. They continually grow and evolve, as they mature into the people they will be as adults. I think our job as parents, mentors, and role models is to make sure those "sponges" have just enough water. With too little, they dry up, starved for the nurturing they need to thrive. With too much water, they drown in the abundance.

> *" ... our job as parents, mentors, and role models is to make sure those "sponges" have just enough water. With too little, they dry up, starved for the nurturing they need to thrive. With too much water, they drown in the abundance."*

The adults in their lives play an important role in helping children develop self-confidence and self-esteem. When they have these traits in the right amounts, they don't shy away from challenges. They stand up for what they know to be right, and they are empowered to make good decisions.

When I see commercials for reality shows like "Toddlers in Tiaras", "Dance Moms", and "Cheer Perfection", my heart aches for these kids. They are being raised to believe that they are only as good as their last performance, that winning is the only way to earn praise. What do you think this does to a child's self-esteem? Why should preschoolers be measured by their beauty—and, even worse, why base the measurement for a child's beauty on adult standards?

Now, picture the parents yelling from the sidelines as their kids compete on the playing field. Whether they're chiding their own children or someone else's, the harsh comments from an adult—like "he's no hitter"—will sting nonetheless. Not every child can be a superstar, but they do shine in their own ways.

When you teach a little girl that she needs to walk, turn, smile a certain way, and wear makeup, she learns that exterior beauty is a strong value. When you push a child to practice, practice, practice in order to be better, you're telling him he isn't good enough just the way he is. In so doing, these little ones are being robbed of the joys of childhood—the freedom to explore, to be curious, to have fun, and sometimes to just say, "I'm tired. I want to stop now."

**❝ *When you push a child to practice, practice, practice in order to be better, you're telling him he isn't good enough just the way he is.* ❞**

To cultivate our children into inspirational leaders with strong values, we need to be sure they know they are loved—and not just by the people close to them. They need to realize that they should love themselves, and develop a strong sense of self-worth that becomes the foundation for so many decisions yet to come.

Without good parental guidance, kids get their self-worth from the Internet, television, music, video games, and social media. These can be very dangerous playgrounds. Video games are violent. Television promotes the importance of vanity, and networks that are popular with teens—like MTV and BET—regularly feature promiscuity. Social media opens up a world of questionable people and activities to young people; even though

Facebook has a minimum age requirement (13), younger kids are finding their way onto that site simply by lying about their birth date. The mere fact that they are being dishonest here is a bad sign of things to come.

Cyber-bullying takes its toll on teens who don't have the skills to handle the relentless taunting. And many of the kids who lack self-esteem become the bullies themselves, because they build themselves up by knocking down others.

Children who lack confidence and self-esteem place too much value in how others see them. They follow role models who are popular, rather than becoming the one to positively influence others. Maybe they try to look and act like the popular kids in school, or some "superstar" that they know only from the public face. If "imitation is the sincerest form of flattery", we should be paying attention to those role models our kids flatter. These children are trying to make themselves into something or someone that other people will admire. Why? Because they don't love themselves enough not to care what other people think.

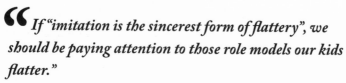 

**"** *If "imitation is the sincerest form of flattery", we should be paying attention to those role models our kids flatter."*

Do you remember the timeless parenting question: "If your best friend jumped off a cliff, would you?" What if that best friend was smoking, doing drugs, having sex, stealing, bullying, cheating, lying, or skipping school? Does your child have the conviction to say "No"? Is she destined to therefore be a follower or will she raise the bar on pre-conceived standards?

We all like to think that our kids can make the right decision when the time comes. To help them along, we need to build (1) their self-confidence so they **believe** in themselves, and (2) their self-esteem so they **value** themselves. We are molding the next generation—*their* generation, not a re-creation of our own. We should maximize who they are, as opposed to shaping them into someone we want them to be. Every child is unique, with his or her own distinct set of attributes, assets, abilities, and strengths. We should recognize and accept the person they are, not dwell on the weaknesses—real or perceived. Emphasizing the negative builds insecurities, while reinforcing the positive builds self-esteem. We should celebrate their strengths, because those are the skills and talents that will inspire others to follow their positive example.

For a child, the process of learning *how* to develop that capability is sometimes more important than actually learning. Does your child learn better by reading or by listening? Once they understand the best way they can learn—for example, by reading, doing, listening—they are better prepared to tackle future lessons.

So, what's the solution? How do you teach a child to "love thyself"? You can start by loving the person they are. Recognize their strengths and praise them. Notice what interests them. What do they gravitate towards? Whether it's sports, art, music, dance, history, animals, space travel, cooking, the outdoors, or some other activity, nurture that spark of interest. If your child is naturally inquisitive, feed that curiosity with games, puzzles, trips to museums, and books—lots and lots of books! In fact, you can never go wrong cultivating the love of books in any child!

**❝ *How do you teach a child to "love thyself"? You can start by loving the person they are."***

Encourage children to recognize their strengths and celebrate them. When your child dresses herself in something out of the ordinary, applaud the fact she took the initiative. When a child paints a picture with a purple sky, appreciate the creativity. Remind yourself that the child is a work in progress and you are there for guidance, not manipulation. When you let a child flourish early on, when you pay more attention to their positive attributes than the negative ones, then you help this young person grow into a confident adult who will be better prepared to handle the challenges of the real world—that place where mom and dad can't jump in and fix the boo-boo's.

# 3 | "Character is the principal ingredient."

When Peter Pan made a promise, he said, "My word is my bond." That was the only assurance that Wendy or the Lost Boys needed, because Peter never made a promise he didn't intend to keep.

Can you say the same?

When a child is whining, "Please! Please! Please!" you might relent just to stop the nagging. Then the promise is made and you either show the child that your word is your bond or prove that promises can be broken.

Conversely, let's say your child promises to clean her room tomorrow if you let her go to a party tonight. In your mind, you're hoping that messy room is clean tomorrow morning—that she doesn't disappoint you—but you know you will have to nag her to do it. Once she has what she wants—permission—the second half of the bargain goes by the wayside.

What do you do? Do you cut her some slack the next day or rouse her out of bed to keep her promise? Or do you kick yourself for not negotiating that the room-cleaning comes before the party??

It's not that your daughter didn't mean what she said at the time. She was probably quite sincere. She also knew that she was telling you what you wanted to hear. Because the promise was made in haste, without thinking ahead to the next day and the chore that lay ahead, there was very little value in the offering.

The French philosopher Jean-Jacques Rousseau said, "He who is most slow in making a promise is the most faithful in performance of it." When we ponder a promise before making it, we're less likely to break it later.

Let me share a story of how a friend of mine, a single mom, handled something similar. Her teenage son had a habit of promising to do the dinner dishes "later". Often, that meant the next day. She didn't like leaving the dishes in the sink overnight, so she ended up washing them late in the evening, before she went to bed. Then she told him that if she was going to go to the trouble of cooking the meal, he could promptly do the clean-up. She insisted that the dishes be done right after dinner.

He whined about how he had to do his homework, so she backed down and told him he had to do them before bedtime.

Still, the dishes were left overnight.

The next day, she told her son that if he didn't do the dishes in the evening, there would be no dinner for him the next night.

When he once again failed to deliver on his promise, she prepared a sumptuous dinner of his favorite—chicken parmesan—but made only enough for herself. One chicken breast, one serving of pasta, and only a small amount of sauce. He stared at her, open-mouthed, as she ate. After she was done, she washed her dishes and put them away. Meanwhile, her son grumbled as he made a microwave dinner.

She told me that he only slipped up one more time after this lesson. She also said that she learned how important it was for her to be precise when making a request or a promise, and that she needed to live up to her side of the deal at all times.

Now, I know many people who regularly make commitments and then fail to honor them. It's an annoying habit. From being late to backing out at the last minute, these missteps chip away at a person's reputation. Yes, they usually have excuses—some are quite valid—but when broken promises become a pattern, the excuses become less and less acceptable.

The Bible says it's better not to make a vow at all than to make one and break it. Making promises because you want to appease someone provides a short-term solution, but long-lasting consequences.

> **"** *Making promises because you want to appease someone provides a short-term solution, but long-lasting consequences."*

As a role model to a child, you must remember that kids have long memories when it comes to holding you to your promise. It's funny how they can forget to make their bed or take their homework to school, but remember a promise you made in passing, weeks ago. We all need a filter in our brain that prevents reactionary promises—those we blurt out without considering what's involved in keeping them. By switching on the filter, there's a pause button before the words can make it from the brain to the mouth. The next time you find yourself teetering on the brink of making a promise that feels a bit wobbly, stop. Switch on the promise filter. Take a deep breath. Pause and consider the ramifications if you offer up a promise. Ask yourself, "What is it I am about to commit to? Is it something I know I can do? Can I deliver on this promise when expected?"

> **"** *The next time you find yourself teetering on the brink of making a promise that feels a bit wobbly, stop. Switch on the promise filter."*

If you have any hesitation, tell the child, "Listen, I would love to make that promise to you, but I need to think about it a little. Let's discuss it later, right after dinner. And I ***promise*** to think about it in the meantime."

When you respond to a child in this way, you acknowledge that you've heard the request and committed to a specific time to discuss it. Being a kid, he might not want to wait. In that case, all you have to say is, "If you want me to decide right now, at this very moment, my answer would have to be 'No', because I need time to think it over. Do you still want an answer right away or will you give me time to think about it?"

Make sure you make yourself available to discuss the request at the time you said you would—because that "appointment" was also a promise that needs to be kept!

If you set this positive example for a child, you're providing a valuable lesson. Just make sure you explain the importance of keeping your word. Talk to the child about why it's wrong to make promises just to get what they want. Teach them how to think past the immediacy of the moment, beyond the burning desire that causes them to make empty promises, Give them examples of when they have been disappointed by a person whose word was not "his bond".

Your positive example will guide your kids to be more careful about the promises they make. They will grow into more responsible, reliable adults. They will earn the respect of other people who know that this person "means what he says and says what he means."

A person who habitually fails to keep his word leaves of trail of broken promises that will eventually become evident to everyone around him. Teach every child that every promise kept is a golden brick that paves a successful pathway.

**❝** *Teach every child that every promise kept is a golden brick that paves a successful pathway."*

# 4 | "Do something because it matters, not because it will get you noticed."

When you want to be heard, you can always find an audience—even if it's an audience of one. But sometimes, great statements require no words at all.

Children need to learn that giving of themselves to do something worthwhile is an investment with the most valuable return—a sense of gratification. That warm feeling we experience after a good deed has a more memorable impact than a tangible prize—which usually ends up tossed in a closet, shoved in a photo album, or spent on something that loses its value in no time.

Yet, children are so often motivated through a reward system that they won't step up to do activities that don't bestow a "prize" on them. They do "extra credit" homework (well, some kids do!), not because they will learn more, but because it boosts their grade or gains appreciation from a parent or teacher. While I certainly have nothing against getting better grades, shouldn't the knowledge they gain be more important than a few more points in the grade book?

Children participate in an event or activity because they will receive a ribbon, medal, or trophy to commemorate their effort, no matter how small. They do chores around the house in exchange for allowance. There is always something to pay them for their effort.

This need for payback is ingrained in them, so they clamor for more recognition—the dangling carrot that entices them to act. Rewards are fine for small children. I know from experience it's essential for some positive outcomes, like potty training. But I also know of parents who essentially bribe their children to get good grades. "If you make the honor roll, I'll buy you a new phone" or "I'll give you $10 for every 'A' on your report card."

What message does this send to a child? Everything has a price or a reward. Why can't personal satisfaction of doing something good, well, or important be enough to receive in return?

If you read or watch the news, you're likely to see all kinds of horrible stories about the human experience. "If it bleeds, it leads" is the prevailing media strategy. Once in a while, buried underneath the disheartening news, there are "human interest" stories of people doing heartwarming things. A family whose home burned down is suddenly inundated with donations, offers of a place to stay, and help with rebuilding their lives. A woman faints and falls into the subway tracks and a bystander risks his life to jump down and pull her out before the train barrels through. Someone sees a mugging take place and chases down the criminal to make sure he doesn't get away with the assault.

Not one of these samaritans was motivated by reward. They acted from a core value that dictates doing the right thing for that reason alone. They're not expecting awards or recognition.

Police officers, firefighters, and our country's armed forces put themselves in harm's way every day they go to work. That's their jobs. They don't expect applause.

For today's children to become tomorrow's leaders, we need to instill in them the importance of doing something because it truly matters, because it will make a difference in someone's life or the world we live in. They should recognize that credit is unnecessary—doing the right thing is its own reward.

*" They should recognize that credit is unnecessary—doing the right thing is its own reward."*

Our culture has evolved into one that relies on volunteerism, community service, and teamwork. People are encouraged to pitch in. It doesn't take a huge effort to make a big impact, particularly if more people get involved.

As a side note here, more and more schools are including community service hours as a requisite to advancing to the next grade. And the courts are doling out community service requirements in lieu of jail time for some criminal offenders. While I appreciate that organizations are benefitting from the assistance provided by the unpaid workers, it's a shame to use community service as a punitive measure. If we can somehow encourage more young people to serve their communities out of their desire to help, we will build a generation that uses their minds, talents, and times for more useful purposes than playing video games, ranting on Twitter, and seeking personal gain.

At the age of eight, Vivienne Harr learned about human trafficking of children and decided to use her summer 2012 vacation to raise money to fight modern-day child slavery. She set up a lemonade stand in front of her Fairfax, California, home and vowed to work every day until she raised $150,000, which she calculated would save 500 enslaved children. The socially conscious youngster used only fair-trade ingredients. In the beginning, she was selling her lemonade for two dollars a glass. Then she decided to ask people to "Pay what's in your heart" and the average price soared to 18 dollars.

In 57 days, Vivienne raised $30,000, which she donated to Not For Sale, a non-profit organization based in Half Moon Bay, California. In 173 days, she surpassed her initial goal of $150,000 as the news media spread the word of her quest. Vivienne is still working for the cause through her online business, Make A Stand! Lemon-aid.

Vivienne believes that everyone should be part of a solution. "Gandhi was one person. Martin Luther King was one person. Mother Theresa was one person. Why can't you be one person who helps?"

There are many other children who are doing the right thing. Yash Gupta has collected more than $100,000 worth of eyeglasses and organized eye exam clinics for students in third world countries. His passion was ignited in ninth grade after he broke his glasses and spent a week in school without being able to see the board. The experience made him think about children who had to go a lot longer without good vision.

Six year-old Raegen Junge made bracelets and sold them to raise money to help tornado victims in Alabama. At eight years old, Adam Claggett started a food drive every Easter and Thanksgiving. Since 2008, he has collected 14,000 pounds of food for the local food pantry in Illinois. And Dylan Ward was so impressed with the nurses who cared for his grandfather during his battle with cancer that he started raising money for Macmillan Cancer Support by selling his paintings. He also collects donations so he can create Wonderboxes, which are toy boxes filled with arts and crafts supplies and games to give to children in the local hospitals.

These are all examples of children who had big ideas, but started small in order to achieve them. They are proof that one person can make a difference, and their achievements should be used to inspire others to follow the same path.

True leadership comes from inspiring other people to achieve their potential, to challenge themselves to do more and go farther than they believed possible. To create this type of leadership in a young person, we need to encourage them to explore the world around them and to recognize that one person can make a difference. When a child sees something that sparks passion or curiosity, we need to do our best to fan those flames. Give them examples of other youth who have created wonderful results, like the ones mentioned here. Help them gather the resources they need to follow through on their good intentions. Be the catalyst that launches a child toward greater things.

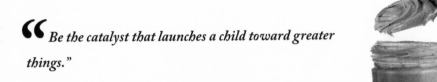

❝ *Be the catalyst that launches a child toward greater things.*❞

A leader also knows that the reward of leadership comes from seeing the success of their followers, students, mentees, etc. It's not necessary to be rewarded for their own role in the achievement of the people they lead. And they certainly don't take the credit, but rather shift the focus away from themselves to the individual or team. In so doing, they are rewarded with the appreciation, respect, and loyalty of these followers. These invaluable gifts, along with the satisfaction of helping others, represent an "income" that we should all strive to earn.

# 5 | "Be thankful you don't get everything you ask for."

Seeing is believing. For kids, seeing is also *wanting*. That's just how they are. They are naturally selfish, which comes from the innate instinct for self-preservation. Infants cry when they are hungry, wet, tired, or need a hug. When their needs aren't met, they cry harder.

From all the enticing things on television to the items within reach in a store, their eyes grow wide with desire. They can't see or think past the immediate want. Money is, of course, no object to them, Mom and Dad take care of those details. When children are very young, you can usually satisfy them with something inexpensive—a Matchbox car, a coloring book, a pack of gum—but the price tag for their wants grows proportionately with their age.

Before long, the cost of satisfying a youngster requires a wardrobe that costs more than your first car! Their technology—smartphone, gaming system, laptop—is outdated before it's even paid for. Do you go into debt to appease the wants of your child? Unfortunately, many people do. But if you teach them from a young age that they should be thankful they don't get everything they ask for, you put yourself and the child in a much better (and financially healthier) situation.

Teach them the value of money. Explain the relationship between wanting something and earning it. Make it a habit for both of you to understand the reason for the object of their desire. Let them know that getting what they want is not a foregone conclusion. Give them the wonderful power of restraint, so they understand the difference between "want" and "need" when making a purchasing decision. Yes, I know, she might truly believe she "needs" those expensive shoes, but in a few weeks, that life-altering item will be just a costly blip on life's radar screen. Teach them these lessons now so that they don't fall into the credit card trap of over-spending. Help them avoid a mountain of debt and a bad credit rating that could prevent them from getting what they truly need.

**"** *Give them the wonderful power of restraint, so they understand the difference between "want" and "need" when making a purchasing decision."*

Kids don't have the maturity or experience to understand what is necessary, or even good for them. Left unchecked, this trait becomes part of their personality. From an economic standpoint, they can't distinguish between the ability to make a purchase and the wisdom of doing so.

I used to have a passion for cars. I really wanted a Lamborghini. That was my dream since I was a child—a shiny, sleek, yellow Italian sports car. As an adult, I owned nice cars, but nothing over the top. Still, I hadn't abandoned the vision of driving down a winding road, revving the engine of my Lamborghini.

One day, one passed my wife and I on the road and I once again voiced my wish. Either because she knew how much I wanted the car or was tired of hearing about it, she asked me, "Can we afford it?"

I thought for a few seconds, running rapid mental calculations, and answered, "Yeah."

"Then go get it," she said, as though we were talking about a new television set, not a six-figure vehicle.

I can't tell you the excitement that rose up in me. At long last, I was going to live the dream!

Then I started to examine the purchase. I thought about the long-term consequence, past driving it from the dealership and down the highway. The business side of my brain kicked in and I thought about the total cost of ownership. People who own these cars do not drive them on a regular basis. They stay in the garage—or the shop. As a high performance vehicle, a Lamborghini needed tender loving care, and it came at a price. I learned that an oil change could run into the thousands of dollars.

Finally, I realized that even if I could afford to buy the car of my dreams, handle its high maintenance and insurance costs, and had the blessing of my wife (that was the most shocking), this expense was not a good use of our resources. A couple of weeks later, I decided against it. To this day, I have no regrets. I think that knowing I could have had the car was enough for me. I would have never enjoyed the Lamborghini to the extent I expected when I was a teenager imagining myself behind the wheel (however, I did take a testdrive)!

Sometimes you have to reach the point where you look beyond what you want, and focus on the aspirations that underscore them. What drives your choices? Most of the time, we're too close to the things that we want and can't see the other issues that are connected to the choice. We need to remove the blinders and show children how to do the same so that they can make better decisions, and then pass that wisdom along to others.

So, how do you do this? Well, let's go back to the "My word is my bond" lesson (#3). Don't waver after you've said "No" to a pleading child. My children know that when they ask me for something and I say, "No", there's no more discussion. Case closed. They also know that my wife's "No" has room for negotiation. I've heard the whining from the other room. When I walk in, they look at me and they know the decision is made. They've learned the boundaries, and they respect those limits because I stand by them at all times.

Our culture promotes instant gratification. We have microwave meals, overnight shipping, high-speed Internet, drive-through liquor stores, texting, self-serve checkout, and a variety of other services designed to allow us to get what we want as fast as possible. With all of these instant possibilities, we need to learn (and teach) restraint. We should all take the time to evaluate our wants and needs before clicking "Send" or handing over a credit card. Living according to the distinction between "want" and "need" will help a young person develop a healthier lifestyle that is less dependent on acquisition and more on core values.

Kids roll their eyes when you give them the "When I Was Your Age" speech. The message here should not be about our sacrifices—raise your hand if you actually walked five miles in the snow, barefoot, to school. We should communicate about consequence so that children can decide for themselves between a "want" and a "need".

# 6 | "When you let money define you, it drowns out everything else you meant to say."

We're living in a world where wealth is paraded in front of us every day. When you Google a famous person, you're certain to see images of celebrities with their mansions, expensive cars, jewels, and designer clothes, while they jet around the world. Watching gala award shows, like the Oscars and Golden Globes, used to be about seeing who wins and loses. But now the media pays as much—if not more—attention to the red carpet parade before the event. Who is wearing what designer's outfit?

And why are they highlighting clothing that 98 percent of the viewers could never afford to buy? Even the stars themselves borrow a lot of the over-the-top jewelry they wear to these events.

The answer is, because so many of these people want to see it. They dream about what they could have with more money. They want to imagine themselves with such lavish lifestyles. They envy the trappings of wealth.

It's wonderful to dream, but when you let money define who you are, that's all that people will see—a shallow layer of dollar signs. Is that a core value that you want to teach your child? How much substance is there to a person who is driven by high-priced possessions? There is no sense of achievement—no finish line—because there are always more things to be bought. There will always be new temptations to spend your money on. Then, you need to spend money just to maintain the image of your high-priced lifestyle. It's like an addiction—not to drugs or alcohol, but to living expensively.

> **It's *wonderful to dream, but when you let money define who you are, that's all that people will see—a shallow layer of dollar signs.*"**

Consider two couples I know. The first one is wealthy. The wife—who comes from a very modest lifestyle—has allowed herself to be completely defined by money. She absorbed a money mindset like water on a dry sponge. At a pool party, she insisted she simply couldn't drink wine from a polycarbonate glass, like the rest of us were doing. Never mind that it made more sense to avoid broken glass in a place where people were barefoot or that everyone at the party was fine with the non-breakable non-glassware. She was inflexible.

The pool was situated a distance from the house, but this woman had to make the long walk to get the crystal because her sensitive palate was so offended by anything less.

I won't even get into the issue with using paper plates, but I'm sure you can guess!

Now, there's another couple who are friends with this first pair—well, maybe more like acquaintances. These people don't have wealth, but they do everything possible to look like they do. They are trying hard to run in the same circles as their genuinely wealthy "friends", and their obsession has put them into serious debt. They are struggling to present the appearance that they are more financially successful than they are. The thing is, people who know them would probably prefer them to be more authentic, to forego the trappings they can't afford, and just be themselves.

Your financial status is only important to other people if you allow it to be. They don't need to know how much money you have; that's your personal business. The way you act toward others should not be affected by how much wealth you—or they—have accumulated. You should accord everyone respect, regardless of the size of the bank accounts.

When children head out to school and jobs, they will interact with people from all social, economic, and cultural backgrounds. They need to be able to relate to people, whether they are financially secure or not. Infusing them with the belief that money makes them special or better than others is a lie. You create boundaries that limit their opportunities to learn from other people outside their fiscal sphere. In addition, this type of elitist principle conveys that a person's true value is measured in dollar signs. If you want to cultivate children into the leaders of tomorrow, you need to start with their self-worth, and that is something that is priceless.

> **❝ *If you want to cultivate children into the leaders of tomorrow, you need to start with their self-worth, and that is something that is priceless.* ❞**

Young people should be encouraged to measure themselves and others by what they *do*, not what they *have*. They need to recognize the importance of being a well-rounded individual. Money can be a fleeting commodity. It comes and goes—the speed at which this happens is largely determined by the individual. I know many people who are just getting by with their paychecks. Then they get a raise and rather than use the extra income wisely and pay off consumer debt, they just increase their spending. Before long, they're back to living paycheck to paycheck.

Self-awareness, empathy, confidence, and self-worth will remain with you forever. And you can't put a price on that.

# 7 | "Money can't buy class."

When I speak to youth, whether it is before a large assembly or a one-on-one conversation, I often ask them about their definition of success. More often than not, they share with me their aspiration to accumulate financial wealth as their number one goal in life. Truth be told, at one time in my life, I had the same outlook. An abundance of money can give a person many things. You can purchase the items and services you want. You have the peace of mind that comes with not worrying about paying your bills or putting food on the table. Financial abundance may also allow you to enjoy your life more fully by taking lavish vacations or even retire early.

But no amount of money can buy class.

People come into money in different ways. They're born into it, they earn it, some luck into it. Most newcomers to wealth have not been schooled in the ways to use it. For instance, many athletes, musicians, TV and movie stars from less than ideal backgrounds suddenly earning multi-million-dollar salaries figure that, "I've got the money, I can do what I want." Often, they waste it on flashy toys, clothes, homes, and more. The problem is, they become role models for youth who see this wasteful, frivolous behavior as indicative of a positive role model.

I know couples who earn more than a million dollars a year, but sometimes their kids present themselves as if they're homeless. Boys walk around with their pants drooping past their posteriors, exposing their underwear. Daughters wear clothing that is far too tight, also exposing more flesh than the public needs to see. Parents let their kids dress in this "style" (and I use that word very loosely) because they want their children to freely express their personalities, somehow fearing that boundaries would either compress their creativity or create anger and resentment. Frankly, I don't buy either of these excuses.

What these young people (and their parents, for that matter) are reflecting is not style, but a lack of class. Sure, the clothing might be from the latest "hip" designer, but a hefty price tag and impressive label does not necessarily equal class.

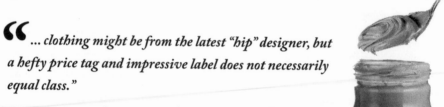

**“** *... clothing might be from the latest "hip" designer, but a hefty price tag and impressive label does not necessarily equal class.* **"**

At the same time, high style means nothing when a person opens his mouth and speaks offensively, obscene, or without any connection to English grammar. Dropping an f-bomb in every sentence will make even the best-dressed person present as "trashy".

Let's be real. I grew up in an environment where young people adapted their vernacular to fit whatever social environment they were in at the time. It was called "survival". The difference today is that youth have not been nurtured in the "principles" that will lead them back on the right course, much like the North Star can return a wayward ship to its destination.

Certainly, you are allowed express yourself, but there are acceptable standards, and it's up to parents, mentors, and other people of influence to communicate the boundaries of appropriateness to youth. Teachers need to be clear about acceptable language and behavior in school. Dress codes should be enforced—at home and in school. I'm not necessarily talking about uniforms, but a presentable appearance. Clothing that fits and shirts that don't scream offensive comments.

In 2004, comedian and education advocate Bill Cosby addressed a group when he received an award from the NAACP. Here's a bit of what Cosby said that day:

*"They are showing you what's wrong. People putting their clothes on backwards. Isn't that a sign of something going on wrong? Are you not paying attention? People with their hat on backwards, pants down around the crack. Isn't that a sign of something or are you waiting for Jesus to pull his pants up? Isn't it a sign of something when she's got her dress all the way up to the crack—and got all kinds of needles and things going through her body? What part of Africa did this come from? We are not Africans. Those people are not Africans; they don't know a damned thing about Africa. With names like Shaniqua, Shaligua, Mohammed and all that crap and all of them are in jail. (When we give these kinds of names to our children, we give them the strength and inspiration in the meaning of those names. What's the point of giving them strong names if there is not parenting and values backing it up)?"*

Cosby's speech got people riled up, then and now. Some people viewed his tirade as elitist, while others vehemently supported Cosby's statement. I believe that Cosby's message is not about race. It's about parenting. Too many adults have failed to define and promote "class" for their children. If they are going to endow their children with possessions, they also need to provide a sort of "user's manual" that gives them guidelines for what's the appropriate way to wear, use, or otherwise manage these toys. It's absolutely reasonable to accessorize a child's cell phone, iPad or Internet access with a detailed agreement about what's proper, acceptable, and safe.

**❝** *If they are going to endow their children with possessions, they also need to provide a sort of "user's manual" that gives them guidelines for what's the appropriate way to wear, use, or otherwise manage these toys."*

I've interviewed young people who have applied for a job with one of my companies, dressed like they would be going out to hang out with their friends. That's fine if you want to work at a video game store or tattoo parlor, but when kids are going to interact with people outside their generation, they need to understand that their sense of style is microcosmic and is seen by others as classless. At the very least, it's limiting their opportunities. That's because most youth don't understand the concept that THEY are the one who needs the job. The company doesn't need them. Therefore, youth need to present and carry themselves as someone the employer sees as representative of its corporate image. It's not about your individuality at that point; it's about the type of person that the company wants the consumer to see as its public face. If you present yourself in any extreme fashion, be it promiscuous dress, indiscrete tattoos, or excessive body piercings, be prepared for rejection. Period. Like it not, you don't control how you're perceived. You can only control how you present yourself.

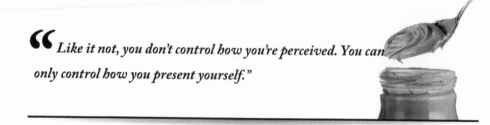

**❝ *Like it not, you don't control how you're perceived. You can only control how you present yourself.*❞**

Many portions of the population are economically better off than they have ever been. But regardless of how much money you make, you need to always represent your self-worth. Don't assume that it goes with your income bracket. Just because you have the ability to buy something, doesn't make you a better person. The money in your pocket doesn't define you as a person of class; your attitude does. I know many young people who come from poverty and they exhibit manners, intelligence, and class. Their parents understand that it doesn't cost a thing to be clean, speak well, and take pride in yourself.

Cosby addressed another audience and he spoke about setting boundaries and giving direction to children. "These are your children. You're supposed to raise them."

Reality TV is a major cause of the disintegration of the social fabric and blurred lines of acceptable behavior in our society today. Most people honestly do not realize that most reality TV shows are highly scripted and edited to convey whatever the producers, network brass, and advertisers want to show, in pursuit of higher ratings. You only need to examine the contract of these reality "stars" to understand that the vast majority are bought and sold for a few pieces of silver, only to lead, however unwittingly, countless viewers down a path of social and ethical destruction.

There's a distinct difference between a culture that is developed over time and one that is living by fads. Before you spend money on supporting trends so your child can appear stylish, invest in their sense of self. Show them what class really means.

# 8 | "Be yourself. Everyone else is taken."

Popularity and "hip-ness" are important to young people. They want to be accepted by others they deem important—whether that's their parents or peers. They are so easily influenced to adapt because they haven't yet developed their own persona, so they're "trying on" others.

This is normal. In fact, it's encouraging when children explore possibilities and try new things. It's so frustrating when your child will only eat macaroni and cheese or is hopelessly committed to one pair of pajamas. When they finally branch out, you're euphoric.

In the early years, a child is trying to find him/herself. Everything is so brand new to them—those bright and shiny objects that are too tempting to resist. You can watch and offer guidance, but it's best to let the child go through trial and error. Some things—like superhero or fairy princess costumes or watching the same movie over and over and over—will just run their course.

Eventually, children wade through the stream of curious and tempting things, and they hold onto those that matter to them. The problem is that "what matters" might not be genuine. Maybe they haven't yet developed the self-esteem and self-worth to confidently adapt the style, behavior, and attitude that truly reflect who they are. Quite possibly, they are mimicking their role models—which could run the gamut from dressing like the popular kid in school to talking like an angry hip hop star who decries everything you hold dear.

You might shrug it off as a phase—and it very well could be just that. As I said, kids need to explore the world around them, try it on, and see what fits. But the most important aspect of this process is that they remain true to their core self.

> *❝ ... kids need to explore the world around them, try it on, and see what fits. But the most important aspect of this process is that they remain true to their core self.❞*

Over the past decade, we've been hearing more and more about the importance of "authenticity" and "transparency". With so much information—and misinformation—being hurled at us from every direction, it's important that we are able to identify what's real and honest. The Internet grants people such anonymity that they can assume any identity they choose. College football star Manti Te'o was involved in a relationship with a woman he met on Facebook in 2009. The two never met but spoke on the phone, but he never admitted this fact to his family, fearing they would be critical. When he was told in 2012 that she had died, he was devastated, and because of his celebrity status, the story made national news and drew outpourings of sympathy for the athlete who continued to play in spite of his heartbreak.

In January 2013, it was discovered that Te'o's "girflfriend" didn't exist. It was a hoax perpetrated by an acquaintance of his—a man. The truth caused tremendous embarrassment to the football player, who was a Heisman Trophy candidate and expected to be a high pick in the 2013 NFL draft. Originally expected to be selected up in the first round, Te'o slipped to a second-round pick, which some people believe resulted from the off-the-field issue with the hoax. The difference between the first and second round can be millions of dollars in salary as well as product endorsements.

Like so many over-used words—"quality" and "value" being prime examples—"authenticity" is tossed about with such thoughtless ease that the meaning has become less, well, meaningful.

Authenticity means being honest, real, and genuine. There is no imitation, no duplication, or false representation. When I see young people covered with tattoos and body piercings, I wonder why they have to work so hard at make a visual statement. Is there not enough substance beneath the surface? When they dress in an outlandish way, why are they craving the attention so badly? C'mon, guys, pull up your pants. There's a reason they call it "underwear". And outfits that look more like theater costumes just remind the world that a person is play-acting.

Famed fashion designer Coco Chanel once said, "Dress shabbily, they notice the dress. Dress impeccably, they notice the woman." You have to ask yourself and your children, "How do you want to be viewed and what does that say about you?"

Individuals who use their appearance as a billboard to scream out a bold statement might be masking the person underneath. Certainly, I'm not saying that everyone needs to dress conservatively or refrain from bold expression or behavior. We need unique individuals who cause us to rethink our norms. But if those people are not genuine, their message is shallow and, therefore, of little value. In fact, they're masking their true identity, not allowing themselves to bloom.

The people who emerge as leaders are those who naturally attract and *maintain* followers. Charisma causes attraction, but authenticity maintains loyalty. When people know they can rely on a person—that the leader's behavior is real and his/her commitment is genuine—they feel comfortable, confident, and trusting.

Steve Jobs was an innovator who led Apple to become one of the world's most trusted brands. Throughout his career, he stayed true to himself. He was known to be hot-tempered and passionate—often exploding at staff during meetings—but neither his genius nor his commitment to the company he co-founded in 1976 (at the age of 21) was ever questioned. Even when he was pushed out of Apple in 1985, Jobs continued to follow his passion for technology, starting up another hardware and software company, NeXT. Although that venture never flourished, Apple bought the business in 1997 and Jobs was welcomed back to his post as Apple's CEO—at his chosen salary of one dollar per year. Under his leadership, Apple revolutionized consumer technology, launching iTunes, the iPod, iPhone, MacBook, and iPad.

Sadly, Jobs died of pancreatic cancer at the age of 56. But no one would ever question his authenticity.

"Your time is limited. Don't waste it living someone else's life," Jobs once said. Certainly, he lived by that principle.

Encourage the children in your life to be honest with themselves. Self-awareness will help them make informed decisions. They will relate better to other people because they project authenticity. As long as they have a strong foundation of valuing who and what they are, young people will not need to blindly imitate or follow others. You can help them reach this point in their growth by helping them to identify their core values, understand the importance of authenticity, and make choices that resonate with them.

# PART

## MAKING WISHES COME TRUE

Children make lots of wishes. From the time they first hear the story of Cinderella or Aladdin, they learn that some people get what they wish for. Your job as a parent or mentor is not to fulfill all of their wishes, but to empower them to make their own dreams come true. You need to help them understand the difference between a wish and a goal—that one is inactive and the other is proactive. Children should learn the value of setting and achieving goals from a young age. From earning an allowance to improving their grades to getting the college acceptance or job of their choosing, they should grasp that the power is in their own hands.

**❝** *Your job as a parent or mentor is not to fulfill all of their wishes, but to empower them to make their own dreams come true. ❞*

In this section, I'm offering you a collection of lessons I learned that helped me to better understand what it takes to identify goals, set a plan to achieve them, and then pursue them with all of my ability.

# 9 | "Success is a verb."

Success is always going to be an action. I don't know any successful person who hasn't **done** something—usually a lot—to get there. They don't sit high on a mountaintop, reigning over their past. They set goals, they make sacrifices, and they keep working when others might give up. Successful people didn't get there by sitting still and "waiting for their ship to come in." That ship has sailed and it's heading for another port!

Most successful people have the next goal ready before they have achieved the previous one. That keeps their brain active, and motivated to take action to make their life better. I'm not talking about amassing wealth either. To some people, being a success means having security in their job or personal life. They have enough money to support their needs and desires. They have found happiness for themselves.

**❝** *Most successful people have the next goal ready before they have achieved the previous one.* **"**

Success is a relative term. You need to determine what that is for you. Define where you're going before you head down that road. What's your vision of a successful outcome? How do you know you're finished? If you don't know where the goal line is, you'll never reach it.

Inheriting money is not success. It's receiving. People who believe they have achieved something as a birthright are merely riding on the coattails of someone else's hard work and sacrifice. They haven't done anything themselves. I don't care whose family the stork dropped you into, if you don't contribute something to your life and your world, then you have failed to maximize the most precious gift you'll ever have: time.

I've seen many more people come from nothing and create success than those who were born into wealth and then carved their own path to success. Maybe it's the hunger for getting something more than you had before or the deep-seeded desire to break through boundaries. Both wealth and the lack of it have boundaries. When you don't have enough, you want more and try to pull away from the limits you've endured. When you have plenty, you are defined by it. People are successful by what they do, not what they have. What you have is yesterday's news. That's what you did in your life so far. Where will you go from here?

**❝** *People are successful by what they do, not what they have. What you have is yesterday's news.* **❞**

When you are promoted in your job, do you stop performing? If you did, you wouldn't last long. When athletes earn championship titles, do they stop there? Is that the mark of a champion—someone who stops when he thinks he has reached the top? For most, they taste success and want more of it, so they keep striving to improve and to build on opportunities. They recognize that a championship title is a fleeting thing that must always be defended and earned again.

Businesses have to keep innovating in order to succeed. They know that the competition is fierce and consumers are fickle, so they build on their past success—their brand—by looking for the next great thing.

Like those achievers—whether an individual, team, organization, or business—you will be applauded for your past successes. But the applause is short-lived. Ultimately, you will be measured by your ongoing performance. Life judges you by what you achieve. When you stop working toward a goal, you slip down the meter. You've wasted time that you will never regain.

**❝** *Ultimately, you will be measured by your ongoing performance. Life judges you by what you achieve.*❞

The people who haven't followed this principle usually arm themselves with an excuse. It's somebody else's fault. Their parents didn't encourage them. They didn't get to go to a good school. They didn't have enough education. The boss didn't give them a fair chance. They didn't have the time or the money. Nobody supported their vision. Blah, blah, blah....

In the end, does the excuse really matter? An excuse doesn't change the reality that you failed to meet your life's objectives. Unlike the game of Monopoly, you don't get $200 just for passing "Go".

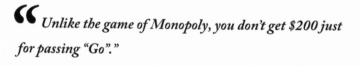

**❝** *Unlike the game of Monopoly, you don't get $200 just for passing "Go".*❞

We tend to value ourselves based on what we think we can achieve. All those visions dancing around in our head of what we are going to do "someday" elevate our spirits and distort the perception of success. It's a mirage.

As I said before, the world judges us based on what we've actually done— not what you say you're going to do or what you promise, but how you deliver. In the end, if you try and fail, you still fail.

Yes, trying hard is essential. However, I also know that there is no standard definition for what it means to "work your butt off". Some people might believe that working extra hours meets that criteria and should be the key to their success. Others believe that hard labor trumps "paper-pushing". It's all in your perspective. Sometimes, that version of hard work leads to success; sometimes, it's not enough. The question is, do you give yourself an excuse and give up or figure out a way to work smarter, not harder?

Putting in hours does not impress me. What impresses me is what you produce, given the same amount of hours everyone else has. Too many people focus in on the effort. Yes, the effort is needed to hone your craft, but you don't get paid on the effort; you get paid on delivering. One of the reasons why professional selling is one of the most highly compensated fields is because there's very little room for excuses. You're not compensated or rewarded for effort, but for results.

It's important to start children at a young age with this idea that success is an action. Help them learn to set attainable goals. Encourage them to learn a new skill—from tying their shoes or dressing themselves to reading a book or reciting the alphabet. Once they have achieved a goal, work with them to find the next pursuit.

# 10

## "The difference between a goal and a dream is a deadline."

For years, you would make a wish and blow out the candles on your birthday cake. Do you remember any of those wishes? Were they important enough for you to do more than hope they came true?

It's wonderful to dream, to open up your mind to possibilities. The problem is, too many people just let those exciting ideas dangle in the wind. They don't grab hold and make a real effort to convert a wish into reality.

How many times have you started a statement with "Someday..."? Did "someday" ever come?

"Someday" is like Neverland. It's out there somewhere, just out of reach. You can visualize what happens there. You lose weight, travel, write a book, pay off all your debt, eat healthier, stop smoking, buy a house, go back to school, move out of your parents' house, and start your own, highly successful business. Wow! I want to live in "Someday", too.

I know the only way to get to this magical place where dreams come true is to chart a course and timeline. Without such parameters, what you call a "goal" is really just a wish. You're waiting for it to come true, when you should *make* it happen.

In particular, young people need to be able to understand that in order to achieve anything, they need a plan with a timeline attached to it. They have to commit to that plan and work it. If they falter along the way, don't give up on the vision. Just adjust the plan. A big part of achieving a goal is motivation, commitment, and tenacity.

Coach Tom Landry said, "Setting a goal is not the main thing. It is deciding how you will go about achieving it and staying with that plan."

When I was a teenager, I used to design things. I would take ordinary household items and convert them for my use. Once, I made a remote control opener for my bedroom door. The key word here is "opener" because I never figured out how to make it close. Anyway, I designed other things like cars and houses. After I grew up and could afford to buy more creature comforts, I decided I would dust off some old floor plans of homes I envisioned I could build "someday". To my surprise, though very rough around the edges, my teenage concepts were very consistent with my 40-something ideals of a "dream home". So I searched locally (in the metropolitan Washington, DC, area) for an architect who could take my vision and commit it to a set of plans that were structurally viable and practical (i.e., cost-effective). I interviewed several architects who told me that "This is a colonial home market", "We don't have much experience in your style of architecture", and "Sure, we know exactly what you mean". Then, the plans came back looking like a modification or their own "box" style. I became frustrated. Unacceptable. I finally found an architect in the Midwest who got it right and, at last, I had my plans! Now, all I had to do was to shop the plans around to the custom builders in the area and— Voila!—I would have my house. Right?

Wrong. No one would touch it. What I discovered was that the dirty little secret in "custom" homebuilding is that builders tend to build what they know, not what you want. Many are good about "modifying" your ideas to fit into what they're used to constructing, but, ultimately, they build "their" house.

Well, that wasn't acceptable to me, so I decided I could do it myself and hire my own sub-contractors.

Here's the thing. I didn't just have a goal of building the house. I had a timeline, because I had sold my other house and had no choice but to get out. Although I would have loved to take my time on this project, the house would never have been completed if I didn't set a very real timeline. It wasn't easy, and there were many days when I kicked myself for undertaking such a lofty goal, but I had the motivation and commitment to see it through. In the end, I created the house I had dreamed of.

Think about all of the ideas dancing around in your head that are aimlessly waiting for "Someday". Grab the one that excites you the most. Write it down. Don't just think about it. Put it on paper. "Write down the revelation and make it plain on tablets  so that a herald may run with it." Habakkuk 2:2

Now, give yourself a deadline. I don't care if it's tomorrow, next week, or next year, but assign a date to achieve that goal. How do you feel? Don't you feel more committed to that vision now?

Now, you know what you want to achieve and when. The next step is to craft the plan to get there. Think in baby steps, because with each one you complete, you get satisfaction, which motivates you to keep going. Assign a deadline for every step. For example, if you want to run a 5K but haven't run before, give yourself smaller goals, like starting with half a mile your first week and adding distance each week. Suddenly, "Someday" is only weeks away!

With this plan and timeline, you have turned a wish into a goal that has a much greater chance of becoming reality. And as you achieve one goal, you have room in your mind to think bigger and broader, to convert more wishes into dreams that you yourself make a reality.

Think about how you can apply this process to the young people in your life. Kids are dreamers by nature. We want them to imagine what could be and to chase those possibilities with all their might. Think back to Vivienne Harr, the little girl who wanted to raise $150,000 to free enslaved children by selling lemonade. She didn't just hope it would happen "someday". She gave herself a deadline of 57 days over her summer vacation. That date was in her sights, and she worked hard every, single day, charting her progress and remaining focused on her target.

No child is too young to follow a goal. If they can't tell time or know the days of the week, help them. Put a digital clock where they can see so if they have a goal of cleaning up all their toys in 30 minutes, they can measure the time. If you're trying to potty train a toddler, let them check off every day on the calendar that they have stayed "dry". Teach kids to understand that time has value so that they can make the most of it.

> **Teach kids to understand that time has value so that they can make the most of it."**

As your child grows, keep discussing dreams and goals. Encourage them to set up plans to make their wishes come true. From saving money to buy their own toys—which get more expensive with each year of their lives—to mastering a skill or overcoming a fear, they will learn that plans, not wishes, come true when they make them happen. And with this empowerment, they can achieve great things!

Goal-oriented people achieve much more in their lives than dreamers. I encourage visionary thinking, but if those ideas never sprout legs, they don't matter. Give children direction for achieving the things they desire, and explain the difference between wishes and goals.

In "Alice in Wonderland", Lewis G. Carroll wrote:

> *"Would you tell me, please, which way I ought to go from here?"*

> *"That depends on where you want to get to," said the Cat.*

> *"I don't much care where," said Alice.*

*"Then it doesn't matter which way you go," said the Cat.*

Wonderland and Neverland were fantasies, but "Someday" can be very real, because it is as much "when" as "where".

# 11

## "No matter which course you choose, there will always be someone who will tell you that you're wrong."

Have you ever been really excited about an opportunity or idea, only to have someone play "devil's advocate" and burst your bubble?

There's always someone who wants to bring you down to earth—or just bring you down. They might tell you they're looking after your best interests or just being practical, and sometimes that's true. But whether they are worried about your choice or want your life to be as limited as their own, these people will throw out reasons to keep you grounded right where you are. Often, they're projecting their own fears and limitations.

A lot of the negativity and criticism comes from the people closest to you, like friends and family. Your inner circle exerts strong influence over your choices because you trust them, but it's important to remember that every individual has his own agenda and perspective.

Everybody has an opinion. It's up to you to decide which ones are worth taking. Parse the good information from the bad. Be careful about whom you allow to influence your decisions. Consider the source. What experience does this person have that's relative to your decision? For example, you probably shouldn't take marriage advice from someone who has never been married.

Explain to a child that, when you make a choice, you are the one who lives with the consequences—from joy to regret—so you need to make the decision that feels right for you. You need the confidence in yourself and your plan to overcome these objections. Certainly, you need to consider them and filter the constructive thoughts from the destructive ones. Respond to the people who offer valuable insight. As for the others, well, smile politely, nod, and ignore them.

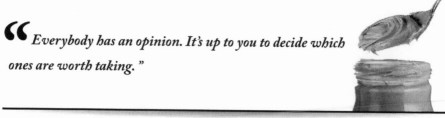

**❝** *Everybody has an opinion. It's up to you to decide which ones are worth taking.* **❞**

Nobody understood why I became an entrepreneur. Some people launch a new venture because of an issue with their current employer or job. They didn't have growth opportunity, wanted to make more money, or just didn't like the job. Others are thrust into the situation by some life event without recourse.

That wasn't my situation.

On the surface, it didn't make sense. I had a solid career, working for a good company, gaining responsibility, making a great salary, and was treated very well by the company and my supervisors. What more could anyone ask for, right? When I told my parents I was quitting to start my own business, they thought I was crazy—and didn't hesitate to tell me so.

"You're making six figures and you're going to just quit?"

I had no complaints, but I knew there was something more I needed to do to feel fulfilled. I had prayed long and hard about my decision to go out on my own. I examined the risks. I had weighed the pros and cons—and the pros won. Ultimately, I had to find and follow my "purpose".

So, I went to my employer and outlined my idea. "This is what I'm thinking about doing. What do you think?"

I didn't get a favorable response, which didn't surprise me. I continued to ponder my plan. Six months later, I went back and told them, "I considered what you said and I'm going to do this any way."

My supervisor told me, "I kinda knew you were going to do that. I didn't want you to leave, so I apologize if I didn't encourage you, but I wish you well."

That company came back to me a couple of years later and offered to mentor my company in a formal mentor-protégé program, which I gladly accepted. Even now, my relationship with them is good.

I had the conviction that I was making the right choice for myself, so I withstood the onslaught of negativity that came my way. Luckily, I had the support of my wife and others, who realized the value of my vision and I was confident that I would succeed.

There will never be a time when 100 percent of the people in your world agree with your choice. Accept that reality. Then you have two choices for dealing with it:

1. Cave in to their opinion.

2. Follow your vision.

Young people don't have the experience and maturity to always make the best choices, so they need your guidance. As they grow, you can help them develop strong decision-making skills by encouraging them to consider options and consequences. Spend time with them to talk about their situation, look at the choices, and weigh the advantages and disadvantages of each one. Sure, they may have already made up their minds, but at least take this step. Explain the importance of *informed* decision-making. Then, even if their decision doesn't work out as they had hoped, they can look back and learn. The more decisions a child can formulate on his own, the more confidence he will develop.

And remind them that not every plan is going to be successful. That doesn't mean your vision is bad. Maybe it was the plan or the execution, or maybe the timing. Nor does it show that you proved those naysayers to be right. You need the intestinal fortitude to work through your plans, stick with your vision, and give it everything you've got. Giving in to the people who just like to poke holes in other people's dreams will cause you to stop taking chances, thinking creatively, and being an individual. Don't let this happen to you or your child.

**❝** *Giving in to the people who just like to poke holes in other people's dreams will cause you to stop taking chances, thinking creatively, and being an individual."*

# 12

## "Talent and intellect does not always add up to success. Perseverance does."

Every so often, I'll come across an article or television broadcast entitled "Where are they now?" I figure that if the question needs to be asked, "they" aren't in the limelight any more. Look at all the child stars who shone so brightly in their youth—Macaulay Culkin, Gary Coleman, and Lindsay Lohan—and seemingly peaked there.

These young people achieved fame early on, without all the effort that others put into their craft. Actor Corey Feldman starred in his first commercial when he was three years old and says he was famous before he even knew his own name. Years later, he battled drug abuse. His best friend, fellow actor Corey Haim, died of pneumonia at the age of 38, after 15 stints in rehab for drug addiction.

Ted Kaczynski enrolled in Harvard University when he was 16 years old. He earned his Ph.D. in mathematics from the University of Michigan and became an assistant professor at the University of California, Berkeley, by the time he was 25. Kaczynski later embarked on a bizarre crime spree that spanned 17 years. Also known as "The Unabomber", he is now serving a life sentence with no possibility of parole for three murders and 23 injuries that resulted from the 16 bombs he set.

Talent and intelligence are not guarantees for success. It's what you do with your abilities that matters in life. Success comes from recognizing your strengths as well as your weaknesses, and pushing yourself to achieve in spite of any obstacles that will most certainly block your path.

There are plenty of talented, smart people in the world. Some of the most gifted people I know (singers and musicians) don't have recognizable names. They love their music, but haven't achieved the fame of many, less talented performers. These artists are passionate about their music and stick with it even when naysayers tell them to quit, that their chosen field is not going to sustain them. They keep going, in spite of the difficulty, because they believe in themselves.

What you find about most people who are successful is that they won't quit. They get knocked down and bounce back up, even when it's almost impossible to find the strength. They learn from their mistakes—but don't dwell on or repeat them.

**❝** *What you find about most people who are successful is that they won't quit. They get knocked down and bounce back up, even when it's almost impossible to find the strength. They learn from their mistakes—but don't dwell on or repeat them.* **"**

The ability to persevere is more important than talent and intellect—and money, for that matter. You just have to be willing to keep going. With every success comes confidence, but even the missteps are valuable. British poet Alexander Pope said, "A man should never be ashamed to own that he is wrong, which is but saying in other words that he is wiser today than he was yesterday."

Comedian and filmmaker Woody Allen professed that, "Eighty percent of success is showing up."

A lot of things I have achieved are not because I was really good, but I was either too dumb or too stubborn to quit—my "dream house" for example. Had I known what it would take to build this home by myself, I would never have undertaken the project. But I had a vision that I just couldn't achieve through someone else—unless I was willing to pay several million dollars to do it.

I wasn't.

And so I felt compelled to see this through, to prove that I was able to finish a herculean task. I had made a commitment to building this house and was not giving up.

The foyer I had designed is round and has a 13-foot ceiling. The crew I had hired to do the framing took longer to construct this small area—which represented about 1/20th of the entire square footage of the house. The carpenters had not followed the blueprints. They did it wrong the first time and I instructed them to tear it down. They refused. . . I had leverage (their money). They got it right the second time.

Yes, there's a line between determination and stubbornness, which isn't bad if you achieve the right result. Leaders need to blaze their own trail and say, "This is what I'm going to do", and then make it happen. We should set up children in an environment where they can be held accountable for their actions. We need to give them challenges, give them tools, and let them work it out. Yes, they'll make mistakes and they'll fall. Like learning to ride a bike, a child will fall, cry, get up and do it again and again, until getting it right. Some people never learned to ride a bicycle because the person teaching them diverted them from the reality that they were going to fall and would have to accept that.

Before becoming a New York Times bestselling author and respected journalist, Malcolm Gladwell couldn't get into graduate school. He tried to get into advertising, but was turned down by every agency he applied to. He pursued a journalism career and worked his way to *The Washington Post* and *The New Yorker* magazine. His insights into business and human nature have provided the fodder for books like "The Tipping Point: How Little Things Make a Big Difference", which Amazon's customers named as one of the best books of the decade; "Blink: The Power of Thinking" was on *Fast Company* magazine's list of the best business books of 2005; and

"Outliers: The Story of Success" was on the *New York Times* bestseller's list for 11 weeks.

In "Outliers", Gladwell presented "The 10,000 Hour Rule". He proposes that to cultivate enough proficiency to be considered an expert in a topic or with a skill requires 10,000 hours of practice, which translates to about ten years. He cites everyone from Bill Gates to The Beatles as examples of The 10,000 Hour Rule. Each successful person whom Gladwell examined had spent about ten years fine-tuning their knowledge and skill. That's perseverance.

Do you have ten years of experience in an area or interest? Or do you have one year of experience ten times because you've "dabbled" and lost your focus? I'm not referring to endurance either. Simply hanging in for ten years will not strengthen your ability. That's the difference between a sentence and an opportunity. A person learning to play an instrument can practice the scales every day, but if they don't expand the lesson, they're stuck in one place. You need to build on what you learn, push forward, and expand your boundaries.

Perseverance is a learned skill. Young people learn it when they see the adults in their lives work through challenges in order to achieve a goal. In the end, you both win.

# 13 | "When you find a problem, always propose a solution—or two."

The easiest thing to do when you have a problem is to look for help in solving it.

That's the easiest thing. I didn't say it was the best.

When your first response to a challenge is to seek others for help, you miss the golden opportunity to develop your own problem-solving skills. Meanwhile, you're strengthening that trait in others. In the end, you become more dependent on others.

As a leader, part of your job is to grow other leaders, not followers. The job of a leader is not to answer every question, but to challenge a person to explore possibilities and find their own solutions. My role in my businesses is to develop my team members into the type of leaders who will fit into my organization—and make it stronger as a result.

I don't have the time—or the desire—to answer every question that comes up, so I provide guidelines, procedures, policies, constraints, regulations, and other such resources that are designed to help them construct an answer to just about any question. The company has a detailed employee handbook, and every new hire must sign an acknowledgement that they have read it. Now, whether or not they actually read the whole manual, well, that's their responsibility to shoulder, not mine. If they come to me to ask a question that is clearly answered in the handbook, I'm not going to be a happy boss. By coming to me with this type of situation, they're showing me that (1) they have chosen to ignore the value of the handbook as a resource; or (2) they aren't confident, skilled, or knowledgeable enough to come up with a solution. Neither of these scenarios bodes well.

The worst thing a person can do is come to me with "I got a problem. How do I handle it?" I then typically say, "What would YOU do?"

How they react shows me whether the person is an order-taker or a thinker. Sometimes, I get a blank stare in response. I then explain that my valued team members are problem-solvers and I "strongly encourage" that skill in everyone.

When I have a group of innovative thinkers and problem-solvers, I don't have to invest my time in doing their jobs, leaving me free to do mine more effectively and efficiently. I don't want to sit here and work out the solution, when that's what I'm paying this person to do.

So, here's my policy. Don't come to me with a problem until you have come up with two or three possible solutions. Think first. Think carefully. And think about the consequences if you come to me empty-handed—because you didn't respect my time enough to put thought into the situation first.

Maybe none of those answers are the solution that fits into the way I'm trying to run my businesses, but at least the effort sparks the thought process rather than throwing the problem into someone else's lap. If you don't know, then that's fine, but don't just come and drop it into my lap without making an effort to untangle the challenge and uncover a potential solution.

Ultimately, every person down the line should understand the culture of the organization and what leadership is trying to convey, rather than sending up problems for others to solve. Once you demonstrate the ability to solve problems, your opportunities will expand. When I was 16 years old, I worked at the King's Dominion theme park in Richmond. I showed my willingness to work out problems myself rather than run to my supervisor. I was rewarded with promotions that gave me immense responsibility and helped me grow my management skills at a young age. By the next year, I was supervising over 200 people. At the time, the promotions, money and prestige were more meaningful, but looking back, it was the opportunity to develop my management and critical-thinking principles that benefited me the most.

**❝** *Once you demonstrate the ability to solve problems, your opportunities will expand."*

You have a wonderful opportunity with young people to build their decision-making and problem-solving skills. When a child is about seven years old, the brain, like the body, experiences a growth spurt in the left hemisphere, which guides logic and reasoning. Before their brains mature, kids' choices are driven by the amygdala, the area of the brain that controls instinctive behavior, such as fear and joy. The frontal lobe is where decision-making happens, and that area doesn't develop until adolescence and beyond.

In a U.S. News & World Report article, "Inside the Teen Brain"[1], neuroscientist Sandra Witelson commented, "The teenage brain is a work in progress."

While the brain is developing, you can stimulate problem-solving by throwing the question right back to your child. "What do *you* think is the answer? How would you be inclined to resolve this?"

**❝** *... you can stimulate problem-solving by throwing the question right back to your child. "What do you think is the answer?"*

---

1    Brawnke, Shannon, "Inside the Teen Brain", U.S. News & World Report,

They might shrug. They might give you an answer you don't like. Or they might take the opportunity to think it through. You can help by directing your child's thinking process, posing more questions about possible directions and consequences of taking them. "Okay, that's possible. Now what would happen if you chose to follow that route? Is that what you want to happen?"

Sure, it's easier to give someone the answer, but in the long run, you're not helping them to build their problem-solving skills. They will keep coming back with their problems, so you're not saving any time by taking the "easy" route. We need to push the knowledge down the chain.

When I was growing up, we didn't have computers and certainly not the Internet. One day, my dad came home with a set of encyclopedias. This whole set was sitting in a bookcase in our family room. Even today, that's an expensive investment. When I had a question, he'd tell me to go look it up. I thought he just didn't want to answer the question, but now I understand, as a parent, that you have to instill children with the tools to solve problems themselves.

I remember a college professor, Dr. Hall, who taught vertebrate morphogenesis (the study of the human bones and muscles). There was a lot of memorization in learning the parts of the body. Dr. Hall was the longest serving professor at the school at the time. She had probably been teaching for more than 40 years by the time I got there. She used to rant to the undergrad students who came through her—now some of the most esteemed and recognized physicians in the country—that the course required a lot of memorization, but we needed to do more than remember the names. We had to be able to interpolate, to take the information and process it to fully understand how everything worked. She told us to come up with a solution to some new problem based on the knowledge she was giving us. I didn't like doing that necessarily, but I understood the whole process of doing research. Today, research has become a whole lot simpler, especially with knowledge-based searches. Just "Google it". You don't have to know a lot. But what do you do if a computer or smartphone isn't nearby, or you don't have a wifi connection? How do you find that information?

We shouldn't shrug off our responsibility to help our children become knowledgeable problem solvers to some faceless source on the Internet. Remember the adage: If you give a man fish, you feed him for a day, but if you teach a man to fish, you feed him for a lifetime.

Feed your children's curiosity when they are young so that they will want to explore the possibilities, tackle challenges head-on, and become independent thinkers. Remind them (and yourself) that parenting is about empowering children to be better—just like leadership.

# 14 | "Confusion is the result of a lack of focus."

It's hard to find quiet time. We're glued to our smartphones, which is like a virtual extension cord connecting us to everyone and everything that wants our attention. And even when you're not getting texts, alerts, emails, calls, and tweets, someone near you is, which is like a secondary interruption. It's easy—and likely—to get distracted.

To succeed in any endeavor, you need the ability to tune out the distractions. If you're one of those people who can't finish one task—like washing the dishes, reading an article, or having a conversation—without shifting your focus to something else, you need to work on managing your attention span. If not, you will not only will leave things undone, but your lack of undivided attention will reduce the quality of those things you do finish (or think you have).

People who don't keep their eye on the target will fail to hit it. You miss a deadline. You fall behind. You don't pay attention when instructions are given so you can't possibly follow them. How many times has your child said to you, "The teacher didn't explain it"? Well, in many cases, the teacher *did* explain, but the child was doing something other than listening.

**❝** *People who don't keep their eye on the target will fail to hit it.* ❞

Then we have these responses:

"I forgot."

"I don't know."

"No one told me."

"I didn't have enough time."

These excuses are signals that your child's focus wasn't where it should have been. From not paying attention to letting the mind wander, lack of focus creates problems that will worsen over time. A missed assignment in elementary school is certainly not a big deal, but what about flunking a college course as a result of failing to turn in a paper on time or, later on, not turning in a business report that leads to a getting fired?

When a person gets in the habit of losing focus, it will snowball, just like any other bad habit.

The lack of focus isn't just reserved for singular tasks either. An individual who doesn't stay mindful of her goals cannot achieve them in an effective or timely manner—if at all. She falls prey to distractions, unable to fend them off. Each time, she pulls up some version of those familiar excuses:

"I forgot."

"I don't know."

"No one told me."

"I didn't have enough time."

Let's be clear. These are excuses, not valid reasons. The real reason she failed to do what she needed was because she allowed herself to lose focus. She didn't place enough priority on the task at hand to remain committed to completing it. Overloaded with stimuli (i.e., interruptive thoughts and activities), she caves in.

I spoke with someone the other day who is always unsure about which way to turn. She can't make a decision. She asks everyone she knows for opinions and then has far too much information to process. These surveys she takes don't provide her with any more clarity—quite the opposite. She just gets more confused.

You probably have someone like this in your life. She asks your advice and then doesn't take it. She tells you, "Oh, something came up and I didn't follow through on that."

This person comes back and asks my advice on another matter. I offer it. Again, she doesn't follow through.

This is a regular pattern with her. She's painfully indecisive and lives in a constant state of confusion. What should I do about my job? Do I still want to live in this place? How should I handle this relationship?

Every time she comes back to me for advice, I am less and less inclined to offer it. Rather than give her an answer to her latest dilemma, I suggest she should focus on the situation, weigh her options, and then make the choice that best fits the outcome she desires. In other words, think for herself!

Then, when she asks me, "What if?" I say, "You tell me."

I think we need to do the same thing with our children in order to help them become more responsible for their lives. Instead of managing every, single detail—activities, assignments, schedules, deadlines—we should hand the job back to them. Think about it. Their lives are scheduled for them. We tell them when to get up and go to bed, what time to be home for dinner, how much time they can spend on the Internet, gaming, or television. Their teachers give them assignments with due dates. We remind them of special plans, like someone's birthday besides their own. We shuttle them from one activity to another—music lessons, dance class, sports practice, scout meetings, play dates. And in the midst of this hectic pace, we just expect them to stay focused.

But when we help them learn to manage their time from a young age, we empower them to be more focused as they grow. Let them determine how many activities are enough. Give them boundaries for the important things—like schoolwork, exercise, family time, and sleep. Talk with them about their priorities—e.g., "Would you rather stick with karate lessons or soccer?"

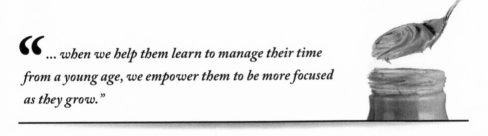

**66** *... when we help them learn to manage their time from a young age, we empower them to be more focused as they grow."*

By helping them pare down their schedules, you're not depriving them of opportunities, but allowing them the ability to focus and really delve into something that matters to them. There are those people who are generalists: known as the jack-of-all-trades and the master of none. But we're in a world where specialization is the key to success. We rely on physicians who have committed to a particular specialty, like orthodontics, cardiology, or pediatrics. If you need a lawyer, you look for someone who has extensive experience in the type of legal counsel you need, rather than a generalist. In everything from hiring a caterer who specializes in kid's parties to a tutor who works only with special needs children, you look for the person who is deeply committed to an interest area.

Your child is not likely to be an Olympic athlete, professional ballet dancer, or concert pianist where they need intense focus and commitment from a young age to succeed. Let them dabble so they can find their passion.

Then help them zoom in on something and stick with it! Teach them that spreading themselves too thin is not a good situation. It leads to doing lots of things, but none of them to your best. Imagine that you have a large garden but only a limited amount of fertilizer. You can either spread the entire area with a very thin layer and hope something grows, or cover just a portion of the garden generously and give those plants a better chance to flourish. How will *your* garden grow?

# 15 | "Overwhelmed is a feeling that always precedes growth."

Not long ago, I had "one of those days". The burdens were piling up at work as I tried to sort through the government shutdown and sequestration cuts that deeply sliced into my business. As the head of the company, I had to organize the tangled mess, so I could make intelligent decisions. I had to take action to make some shifts, but the growing weight of the pressure was taking its toll on me. While I struggled with this additional burdensome task, I also had my normal weight of day-to-day management responsibilities.

During times like these, even the smallest issues are large enough to tip the scale and make the whole pile of "junk" come toppling down. So, I was trying to juggle it all—keeping all those balls in the air—while also sifting through and locate the issues that needed my immediate attention.

Every "quick question" that someone approached me with, every "this won't take long" and "would you mind...?" was adding weight to my mental toughness scale. Those people who sought my attention believed their requests were solitary and seemingly simple. They couldn't see it in the broader sense of it all.

And, you know what? They don't need to. It's not their job to anticipate my work or stress level. As a leader, it's my job to handle it the best I can.

So, in the midst of the frustrating mass of tangled stressors, I stepped back. I took a deep breath and stopped focusing on the large obstacle directly in front of me. It was blocking my view of what lay beyond.

I sat back, closed my eyes, and prayed for clarity of what was waiting for me—and for my company—on the other side of this struggle. My parents taught me at an early age that, when I don't know what to do, retreat to the faith that they had brought me up with, and so that's what I did.

What I realized was that the challenge I was facing—and the overwhelmed feeling it created in me—was the "storm before the calm". There was opportunity in the midst of my angst. I just had to empower myself to see it. As they say, when one door closes, another one opens. I began to consider my options for expanding my market. What untapped niches were out there? What new avenues in terms of services could I be adding or changing in my company in order to not just survive the current onslaught, but to thrive as a result?

I also looked more carefully at my operation. It had been running profitably, so I didn't take the time to examine certain processes and decisions. In times of a recession, people need to work smarter, not harder. I considered a variety of options for streamlining my overhead, without cutting staff. I challenged my management team to do the same, and to work with their team members to find solutions.

I divvied up the responsibility for finding the solution by breaking down the big problem into smaller ones. I discovered that the weight was gradually lifting off my shoulders. That almost paralyzing sense of being overwhelmed parted like clouds. Yes, ultimately, the choices are mine to make, but I realized that I didn't need to make them in a vacuum, apart from the people who have integrally contributed to making my business a success.

I wasn't unburdened of my angst because I had doled out assignments, but because I opened my vision to see more than the troubles in front of me. Instead of feeling the heaviness of negativity, I shifted it to the positive side. My glass was no longer half empty, but half full, and I had the power to replenish it!

Motivational speaker Jonathan Lockwood Huie observed, "Feeling overwhelmed by apparent demands on our time is like going to a restaurant, ordering everything on the menu, and complaining about indigestion."

> **Feeling overwhelmed by apparent demands on our time is like going to a restaurant, ordering everything on the menu, and complaining about indigestion."**

I guess I truly had bitten off more than I could chew—rather, it seemed like it had been force-fed to me. I broke it into smaller, digestible bites.

The bigger the goal, the bigger the challenge, and that adds up to a heavier burden that will undoubtedly load up the stress. You feel overwhelmed when you look at the mounting pile of things to do. But when you can break them down to baby steps that are more easily achieved, you can prioritize the tasks. Basically, you shift the weight around. You shuffle some over there, in the "to be done next week" pile. You off-load some to the "tomorrow" list. You create a "quick and easy" list of things that are clogging up your brain but can be completed quickly, with only a little effort and focus. And you delegate. Good managers are masters at delegating.

Sometimes, it's not that you try to do too much. Maybe you simply have too much to do! So, the answer is simple. Whittle away at that list. Do less and do them better.

> **Sometimes, it's not that you try to do too much. Maybe you simply have too much to do! So, the answer is simple. Whittle away at that list. Do less and do them better."**

I'm sure you've had experiences like this when you were overwhelmed. You felt helpless to make sense of everything and find the right path to the solution. Your head was pounding and you couldn't see daylight.

Stop and focus. Give yourself a time limit to tackle a task. Maybe that's a one-hour attack on your "Honey Do" list at home, 30 minutes of time focused solely on reviewing your budget to find cost-cutting opportunities, or even 15 minutes dedicated to talking with your child without any interruptions. Create blocks of power focus time. Distraction leads to inaction, which causes your burdens to mount.

Remember that it's easier to transplant a seedling than to wait until it has grown into a tree!

**❝** *... it's easier to transplant a seedling than to wait until it has grown into a tree!"*

I now acknowledge that when I reach the point that I am overwhelmed by life, I'm usually heading into a new phase of growth. Just like growing pains in a child occur when their bones are growing and muscles stretching, we experience similar problems when the weight on our shoulders gets heavier and heavier. You have to decide whether you are going to carry the burden yourself or tack action to lighten the load.

**❝** *... when I reach the point that I am overwhelmed by life, I'm usually heading into a new phase of growth."*

Some of that burden is worry—worrying about what **might** happen. Your mind races ahead into all sorts of scary scenarios, which increase the stress. You're better served to identify the "what if's" and push them aside. They are distractions that take up valuable brain space. Yes, you will need to weigh the pros and cons of decisions, but when you dwell in the dizzying space of what might possibly happen, you make no progress.

Another reason you're feeling overwhelmed is because you've allowed self-doubt to creep in. You're so wracked with worry that every decision seems critical, and if you choose wrong, everything will come crashing down.

A bad decision is better than none at all. At least it shows action! Analysis paralysis will not just keep you stuck in place, but could actually push you backward.

Kids today get overwhelmed—and rightfully so. They are over-scheduled with after-school activities, like sports, dance, clubs, music lessons, and other obligations. Somewhere in the midst of all that, they need to find the time for their studies. With so many tasks swirling around in their young minds, how can they sort through it all to create and focus on priorities?

In addition, they are physically weighed down by backpacks chock full of books and binders. I see kids who weigh about 70 or 80 pounds hauling a 25-pound backpack. Put it in perspective. If you weigh 150 pounds, would you be comfortable carrying 50 pounds on your back?

Are we trying to boost the chiropractic industry?

If we want our kids to handle weighty burdens in the future, we need to prepare them now. Teach children how to set aside the fretting and focus on solutions instead. Remind them that this overwhelmed feeling is a growing pain. It's a sign that they have reached a crossroad where they must make important decisions that will help them become stronger and better able to cope.

*" Teach children how to set aside the fretting and focus on solutions instead. "*

I do believe the saying, "That which doesn't kill me makes me stronger." Dealing effectively with challenges and stress is the equivalent of mental calisthenics that strengthen our coping muscles, decision-making skills, and ability to prioritize and delegate.

If you recognize being overwhelmed as a growing pain, you can take it as a signal to step back and sort through the mess in front of you. Help your children do the same and we'll cultivate a culture of happy, healthy, balanced individuals who are far more productive.

# 16 | "Faith makes all things possible, not easy."

My Christian faith has always played an integral part in the successes I've experienced in my life. The principles I was taught and have tried to adhere to these many years have developed my character, my system of values, and a foundation for the way I do business.

Scripture tells us that all things are possible through faith, and I hold that belief in my heart and mind every day.

I'm not just talking about saying a prayer and then sitting back, waiting for something to happen. Nor am I referring to people who spend an hour a week in a church and call that "faith". Yes, they may be able to recite passages from the Bible, but they don't integrate them into what they do and how they treat people.

In truth, even an atheist has faith—faith in the belief that no God exists. It's a negative belief, but one, nonetheless.

When you instill the importance of faith in a child, you empower them with an inner strength that will help them move forward, in spite of the obstacles. They will understand how to measure risk. For example, when I'm playing with my kids and I throw them up in the air, they have faith that I will catch them. They know that Daddy will be there to protect them. They don't share that faith in other people who have not proven themselves.

I want my children to recognize the importance of faith, not just follow blindly. I want them to know that that faith can make all things possible, because I believe it can. You've probably heard about the Laws of Attraction, and positive belief is among them. Visualizing something as possible and "speaking it into existence" can be a strong force toward creating reality, rather than just hoping it will come along.

> **I want my children to recognize the importance of faith, not just follow blindly. I want them to know that that faith can make all things possible, because I believe it can."**

Think about this. If you don't have the conviction in your faith, you're perched precariously, without a solid foundation to support you. As a result, you can be indecisive or even unstable. Anything can come along and knock you down. If you have faith, you can rely on it in challenging situations. Faith can fuel a person to stand up and take action, even when they have endured one setback after another. A person loses his job and then his home and maybe even his family, but with faith, he fights back because he still has the inner strength that won't allow him to quit—the faith in something he can feel, even when he can't see it. His faith doesn't waiver. He keeps pushing ahead and adhering to the principles that he has held for a lifetime.

Certainly, living with faith can be tough at times, particularly when it is challenged. Any sort of guidelines you have in life—rules, regulations, laws, policies, procedures—are designed for a purpose. They're not meant to make life easy for you, but to provide boundaries to protect you—from yourself as well as others. We have speed limits and traffic lights to make the roads safer to travel. We have safety restrictions on amusement rides to prevent injuries. We even set bedtimes for our kids because we know how much sleep they need in order to function effectively and stay healthy.

A system of faith requires guidelines—the rules that dictate what is right and wrong. Children need to explore their expanding world, but we must protect them by providing boundaries—so that they know that they will be caught when they fall.

Children will thrive when there are boundaries to protect them when they take a wrong step. I teach my children the importance of respecting boundaries. When they question one, I ask them to think about why that rule exists. We also talk about when it's okay to step outside those lines.

Faith is the same way. It's a way of protecting you. It's a system that has been developed over time and was put into place to ultimately help you. You have to trust in your faith, and be confident that it will serve and guide you. Whatever you believe, you should know why you maintain that belief. If not, then you are either following blindly or not at all, but merely giving lip service to a faith that really doesn't exist.

When I'm gone, I want my children to be able to make good choices. I hope that they can hold fast to their faith, as I have tried to do, throughout my life. When we teach our children to live a Godly life, they have somewhere to go when we're not there to tell them what to do. Singer Morris Chapman wrote a song that encapsulates this concept,

I may not always be there
To take you by the hand.
I may not always be there
To listen or understand.
I may not always be there
When life seems all uphill.
But I know someone who always will

I may not always be there
To hear you when you cry.
I may not always be there
To wipe a tear from your eye.
I may not always be at your bedside
All the times when you're feeling ill.
But I know someone who always will.

I know someone who always will.

Jesus will always be there
He knows how much I love you,
And in every situation
He'll be there to see you through.

I may not always be there,
But let your heart be peaceful and still,
For I know someone who always will.
His name is Jesus.

As part of my faith, I truly believe that you reap what you sow. When you are good to other people, you will be rewarded with kindness. When I treat people with respect, they do the same to me. What you invest will come back to you—maybe not immediately, but my faith assures me that it will happen. This is an important lesson for children, who desire instant gratification. They need to learn that good things may take time, and may need to be cultivated in order to weed out what you don't want or need.

With faith, we can take chances and expand our horizons. Like my children being tossed up in the air, we believe that someone will catch us when we fall.

PART

# THREE

## THE SCHOOL OF LIFE

Many people believe that "experience is the best teacher" because it allows the student to feel the direct consequence of their actions in "real time". However, I believe that experience, at best, is an inefficient teacher. Principles are the best teacher, because once a principle is learned, the application becomes relevant throughout a person's life and through many different circumstances. *Peanut Butter Principles* stick with you your entire life, and if you allow them, they will help to build the character necessary to lead others.

We spend almost our entire youth in school where we learn a wide variety of lessons—from academic to social. We collect all the knowledge that our elders have deemed we need in order to live better lives and become good citizens of the world. But education doesn't begin and end in a classroom. Principles provide the relevancy between what we are told, what we accept, and what we remember. For example, we learn about fractions and percentages in math class, but until we're trying to figure out the discount on an item, how to divide a cookie evenly between three kids, or how much to tip a server, it might just seem frustrating and irrelevant to our lives.

The "wisdom of the ages" reflects a vast amount of life experience that is invaluable to those people who have yet to learn the life lessons that simply can't be taught in school. And, frankly, that's not the job of those educators. It should fall in the hands of parents, grandparents, and other mentors who pass along such golden nuggets from generation to generation. Here are the ones I've found most helpful.

# 17 | "If you're not early, you're late."

When I share this phrase with people, I usually get a curious look as they figure it out. Sometimes I'm talking to an employee who thinks arriving in the parking lot at the time we are starting our workday means she's on time. Sometimes, I'm reminding my kids as they're running out the front door to catch the school bus as it is just about to pull away from the end of the driveway.

Lateness shows lack of respect and courtesy for the people you keep waiting. What you're subconsciously saying when you're late is that your time is more important than theirs, so people shouldn't mind waiting for you.

I know we're all racing the clock on a regular basis, but punctuality should not be the victim—at least, not habitually. When you are running late, it means that someone on the other end is left waiting or something will either be undone or rushed. None of these scenarios should become habit because the behavior will impede your success. People will learn they can't count on you, which reduces the opportunities you will be given—from invitations to job promotions.

Anything that you want to achieve has a degree of punctuality, including goals. If you set an objective with a timeline, but you're "running late", you just postpone your success. I've found that punctual people tend to achieve more in the same amount of time. They're focused on what they need to do and in what time frame. They tune out distractions and make every effort to stay on task. If you look at a person who is regularly punctual for appointments, you'll see someone who also tends to meet deadlines and fulfill promises. A lot of what we occupy ourselves with is just distractions. Being timely forces you to prioritize those things that are most important.

You can't do everything you want to do and still be timely. People aren't punctual because they let other distractions get in the way.

> *If you look at a person who is regularly punctual for appointments, you'll see someone who also tends to meet deadlines and fulfill promises."*

A friend of mine was telling me about her sister, a chronically late person. Her family knows that when Joan communicates her arrival time, they usually add two hours, or more. For family weddings, there's a standing bet on whether or not Joan will walk down the aisle before or after the bride.

Ironically, Joan, a real estate agent, hates to be kept waiting! She was complaining one day when a client was a half-hour late. She went on and on about all the things she had to do and how appointments were made for a reason.

My friend—her sister—listened quietly and then responded.

"Really??? That's so rude when people don't show up on time, isn't it?"

Joan blurted, "Yes!" and then stopped herself. Her sister was standing there with arms folded, one eyebrow raised, and giving her the look of a disapproving parent. The message was delivered, but will it make Joan a more timely person? Not likely. Joan is one of those people who tries to squeeze in "one more thing". She attempts to pack so much into one hour that she doesn't finish things, rushes through them, or inevitably runs late.

Part of the problem is that people just accept that Joan will be late and they factor it in whenever an activity involves her. They count on one truth: that they can't count on her to be timely.

Do you want to be known as a late person, with that character flaw?

I have a personal pet peeve for crowded waiting rooms at doctors' offices. When I make an appointment and arrive on time, I expect that the person I am meeting should be prepared to meet with me. However, healthcare practices are so intent of making sure that they fill every possible slot in their schedules that they overbook. The assumption is that a certain percentage of people will be no-shows, and the practice does not want to lose revenue, so they believe it is acceptable to book multiple patients for the same appointment time.

Essentially, this says that it's okay for the patient to sit and wait—and wait and wait. The practitioner doesn't even attempt to make you comfortable by giving you up-to-date reading materials, maybe bottled water, and comfy chairs. So, you come to a doctor because, presumably, you're not feeling well, and then you have wait until "the doctor will see you now." This is the ultimate statement of "My time is more important than yours."

And it's wrong.

Even things that aren't as "important" as doctor's visits irritate me with the lack of regard "professionals" have for their customers. When I got married, my wife, who was living in another city until our wedding, moved to my town. She had no local connections and needed a local stylist to do her hair. Because my friend, Pam, was a very popular cosmetologist in the area, I referred my wife to her. In short order, I found out that my wife was spending more and more time at the salon, not getting her hair done, but *waiting* to be seen. No, that is unacceptable, and I strongly insisted that my wife find another stylist. Unfortunately, Pam probably hardly missed her business, because, as I understand it, that sort of disregard is common in that field.

Habitual lack of punctuality indicates a lack of concern and respect for others. Many people simply do not attempt to be on time. They feel that they need to make an "entrance", and God forbid that they are the first to arrive at a party. Ultimately, the inability to manage your life in such a way as to be punctual is a self-esteem issue. These individuals believe everyone should wait on them, because they are more important than anyone else. Not.

# 18 | "Never be afraid to take on the tough jobs."

Wouldn't it be great if the easiest solution were always the best one? And pizza was a health food?

Somehow, I think if pizza were good for me, I'd probably stop enjoying it.

As for the easy way out, well, I would feel like I wasn't getting anywhere if I didn't need to put forth an effort to achieve my goal.

Given the choice, many kids would take Basket-weaving instead of Algebra, and they'd do just the homework assignment, not the extra credit work or "suggested" reading. This is enough to get by. But "good enough" isn't great. It's average. And a "C" grade is average. Are you satisfied with being a "C" student who grows into a "C" adult?

No one wants to do things the hard way, and that's fine when it works. Over-complicating a solution is just a waste of time. But I see young people investing more energy into finding shortcuts than tackling challenges. The time they spend whining about a situation could have been used to deal with it. "But that's soooooo hard!"

Left to their own devices, these children will choose the easy courses, the easy instructor, and the easy way out—every single time. As a result, they don't learn as much as they could—or *should*—and these shortcuts prevent them from exploring their true potential. They don't experience the gratification that comes with mastering a challenge or achieving a goal that seemed unattainable. They just keep living with the bare minimum—average.

A successful person has to move beyond such a complacent attitude. A true leader goes as far as he has to in order to make a difference and achieve something important. He tackles a challenge with vigor and enthusiasm, recognizing that he will gain something from the battle—even if he doesn't win. He'll feel good in knowing that he put forth his best effort and will recognize where he can improve—even if he *does* win. Legendary football coach Vince Lombardi once said, "Winning isn't everything, but the will to win is everything."

> **"** *A true leader goes as far as he has to in order to make a difference and achieve something important. He tackles a challenge with vigor and enthusiasm, recognizing that he will gain something from the battle—even if he doesn't win."*

Earlier, I mentioned that when I was 16, I landed a job working at King's Dominion, a theme park near Richmond, Virginia. The park hired about 2,000 teenagers every summer to work the peak season. I worked in merchandising and games, the largest single area of the park, with 200 employees. I immediately saw that there were opportunities for advancement, even with seasonal employment.

When there was an opening in first line management, the company looked to the seasonal employees. They were eager and, quite frankly, worked for less money than the year 'round staff (whom we called "grown-ups"). I showed that I was willing to work longer and harder. When they needed to juggle schedules, I was happy to come in early or work later, and I willingly took on tasks that weren't in my job description. Soon, I was offered a position as supervisor. Not long after that, I was managing over 200 people. They invited me back the next year, and I was given even more responsibility. Had I been satisfied with doing the bare minimum that was expected, I never would have had the chance to gain management experience from such a young age. I view this job as a major "aha" moment for me. While I hope I'm not vain enough to claim that I was the perfect supervisor at the ripe old age of 16—after all, there were an awful lot of 16 year-old girls who looked to me for "guidance", but I digress—nonetheless, I recognize that I never would have been given the opportunity had I not demonstrated my willingness, and, in fact, desire to take on the tough jobs.

I had another friend, Ricky, who worked at King's Dominion with me. Ricky worked hard and also earned a management position at the park during high school. He went on to play college basketball, and did well. He eventually combined his love for basketball with his management skill and became an acclaimed major college basketball coach.

Ricky and I were both raised with the Peanut Butter Principle, "Never be afraid of taking on the tough jobs"—and it paid off.

If you want to encourage a youth to be more motivated, elevate the expectations. Don't allow them to "just get by". Don't reward them for effort that is less than their best. You can start by providing a good example. Show a willingness to go above and beyond, and demonstrate that a job well done is its own reward. Before your kids take on a new challenge, help them to examine what's involved in doing it right, so they understand the expectations. "Washing the dishes", for example, can also mean clearing the table, properly storing leftovers, wiping kitchen counters and stovetop, and sweeping the floor—not just putting dirty dishes in the dishwasher. However, if you don't communicate those expectations to a child, he isn't prepared to complete the chore.

**❝ *If you want to encourage a youth to be more motivated, elevate the expectations.* ❞**

When we teach children that learning is part of the fun, that rushing to completion is not the intent, we communicate that quality is the goal. We need to do a better job of preparing children for interim successes, giving them a sense of accomplishment along the way to encourage them to keep going. Of course, going overboard turns them into Pavlov's dog, where they perform only for the reward, so there needs to be balance here. Create short-term goals that are attainable and can keep them moving toward a larger goal. If you wanted to lose 50 pounds in a year, for example, you would pace yourself and plan on losing about four pounds a month or a pound a week. Do the same for your children. Take a large goal and break it into smaller goals.

> **" When we teach children that learning is part of the fun, that rushing to completion is not the intent, we communicate that quality is the goal."**

When creating these goals, don't place adult expectations on a young person, because you set them up for frustration, disappointment, and failure. Instead, encourage them to stretch a little farther with each challenge. When you're teaching a child to walk or swim, you don't start by putting them at a great distance away and expecting them to go the distance all at once. You want to be there to catch them, so you stay close and then keep stepping back as they get nearer. Then, when you pick them up, you turn around and show them how far they've come. You celebrate that victory together. Think about how excited a child is when she sees that she walked, swam or rode a bike farther than she thought possible. Creating challenges should be done with the same strategy. See how far they can go and then urge them to go farther. Bring them along with encouragement and support. Don't push them ahead of you where all they see is a long distance.

A child who is self-motivated will grow into an achiever who thrives on results as well as enjoying the journey. Encourage them to avoid shortcuts. And lead by example so that one day, they can do the same for others.

# 19 | "If you're not learning, you're not alive."

When you're a kid in school, it feels like the end of the semester will never come. You attend classes, do your homework, take tests—all with the goal of reaching the end of the school year. Then you count how many more years of schooling are still ahead of you.

It seems like an eternity. And in the scope of a young life, I guess those years do look like a huge mountain to climb.

Then you graduate and look back down that mountain and, in retrospect, it wasn't all that massive. While you're sitting on this summit looking back down to where you started, everything is possible. The cloudless, blue sky is overhead and you celebrate reaching this summit. In all the euphoria, you might not see that Mount Everest is looming in front of you, posing an even higher ascent.

Education never ends. Your classroom time will, but if you want to lead a life that continues with this spirit of wonder and achievement, you will keep your mind open to new ideas and embrace every opportunity to learn. Think of your car as a moving university, and listen to audio books whenever you're traveling. Take part in workshops, seminars, and webinars. If you spend an hour or two in a webinar or workshop and you gain one valuable tip that you can apply to your life or your work, that's a huge return on your investment.

Go to the library or local bookstore and wander through the stacks. Pick a section you've never explored before and see what knowledge is there for the picking. When your child asks you an intriguing question or shows interest in a new hobby, take him or her to look through books to find answers and inspiration. Show them what's possible with knowledge, skill, and practice. It's never too early to inspire a love of books in children! When you teach them that the wisdom of the world—fact and fantasy—is archived in these wonderful books, you give them a priceless tool for lifelong learning.

> **"** ...f you want to lead a life that continues with this spirit of wonder and achievement, you will keep your mind open to new ideas and embrace every opportunity to learn."

Why does this matter, aside from gathering information?

A person who knows "how" will always have a job, but the person who knows "why" will always be the boss. It's more important to **understand** the facts, to be aware of the thinking that goes into the result, than to just have the answer. Otherwise, you're just memorizing, like cramming for an exam. You might know you've got the right answer, but don't know why. Eventually, because the information hasn't sunken in, that knowledge will be forgotten.

> **"** A person who knows "how" will always have a job, but the person who knows "why" will always be the boss."

I think that one of the reasons that so many people don't have sharper math skills is because they were allowed to rely on calculators from a young age. How do you think they'd fare as a cashier if the cash register didn't calculate the correct change for them to give? Try this: If you have a $16 total, give the cashier $21 and see if he knows what to do. I can't tell you how many times, I've had that person automatically hand me back the dollar bill. I push it back and say, "No, I'd like a five in return."

They don't **understand** how to calculate because they haven't had to do it on their own. We're not helping elementary students—particularly as early as third grade—by giving them calculators. Seriously? Does third grade math require a calculator? Shouldn't these young minds be encouraged to figure it out using their own minds before resorting to this crutch?

If you're not growing, you're stuck in one place. Your feet and your brain are cemented there. You're not progressing, not seizing opportunities to expand your world. In nature, look at a flower. If it's not growing, it's not alive.

Let me just state that growth doesn't necessarily mean getting bigger. In the winter, you can't see the grass growing. If you're living in the snowy north, you can't see the grass, period. But beneath the surface, the roots are growing. So, if you're trying to get a nice looking, green yard above the ground, you have to think deeper. For the roots to develop during these colder months and be ready to sprout in the spring, the best time to plant grass seed is in late summer. Then, when it gets hot, the roots are farther down in the ground and the grass has the foundation to sustain itself in the hot summer. If you wait till spring to plant, the young grass will burn up in the summer sun.

Your growth might be slow and you might not be able to see it, but as you attain more knowledge, you strengthen those roots. Give your mind the time and conditions it needs to sink in, and nurture it along. When the time comes that you need the knowledge—from a simple fact to a useful skill, like fixing a leaky faucet or changing a tire—you can harvest it.

A good leader always focuses on achieving knowledge. He seeks answers before the questions are asked, so he continually prepares through learning. He uses his growing mental library to make adjustments as necessary, integrating new information into old plans. He recognizes that no matter what he has achieved in life, his lessons never end. Education is not an end unto itself. It's a tool to unlock, unleash, and empower you to contribute to your own growth and the world around you.

> **Education is not an end unto itself. It's a tool to unlock, unleash, and empower you to contribute to your own growth and the world around you."**

And the smart person knows whom to turn to for knowledge, information, and advice. A person who has failed in relationships is not the one to offer useful advice on the subject. Someone who has been waiting around for the right job should not be influencing your career direction. And even those people who have gone through challenges may not be the best ones to give you advice. Look at their choices, outcomes, and lives. If it doesn't align with yours, think carefully before absorbing their perspective into your decision-making and knowledge base.

A good teacher—and I mean anyone, not just the professionals in the classroom—is so impassioned by their subject that they excite others. They make learning fun. If you want to instill a love of learning in a child, make it fun! Show them how the lesson relates by putting it in a context they can appreciate. Blend storytelling into the mix. When they're studying history, get them to imagine what their life would be like during that time in the past or in a different culture. For science, go online and look up experiments you can do at home together. Read together. Listen to audio books together. Finding an enjoyable and effective process for learning is more important than any lesson.

Curiosity should never leave you, because complacency will take its place. You'll be content with everything the way it is, unaware of what could be. Stay hungry for learning. Ask "Why?" and encourage your kids to do the same.

**❝** *Curiosity should never leave you, because complacency will take its place.* "

# 20 | "Don't worry about what you don't know. Do what you know."

"You learn something every day."

On some days, what you learn is useful and changes the way you live your life—like discovering that eggs don't impact your cholesterol. On other days, your lesson might not be earth-shattering, like finding out that the average baseball in a major league game is used for only 12 pitches. There are useful lessons and fun facts. But when you keep your eyes open, you **will** learn.

John Michael Montgomery wrote "Life's a Dance" and his lyrics have a good message:

> *Life's a dance.*
>
> *You learn as you go—*
>
> *Sometimes you lead,*
>
> *Sometimes you follow.*
>
> *Don't worry about what you don't know.*

You should always be learning (see #19), because fresh information is like fertilizer for your brain. It stimulates and grows your knowledge base. But in your quest to expand your knowledge, broaden your skills, and improve your world, don't overlook the importance of what you already know. You have massive stores of information that you have gathered from your unique life experience. No one else has the same collection as you—or the same perspective.

Two people can look at the same picture and see different things. If you're a gardener looking at a photo of flowers, you see plants that have meaning because they are familiar. Maybe you've read about the species or cultivated them. You may know their Latin names and can list off several varieties. Someone without a green thumb might look at the flowers in the photo and see pretty colors. The same picture might trigger an emotional response from yet another person who associates flowers with a loved one who has passed.

So, you should appreciate that one-of-a-kind font of knowledge you have gathered—not worry about the gaps you perceive. You will never, ever know everything you want or need to. It's just not possible. And you'll just drive yourself crazy trying. People who are so busy trying to gather up information like a starving individual at a buffet are information gluttons who are missing the point. *Use* what you know. Don't take it in and cling to it like a hoarder.

Read a book and then share what you've learned. Don't keep it to yourself. Go online and post a review. Or pass the book along to someone who could benefit from the content. So, what are you doing to celebrate what you know? Are you treating people to your cooking or baking talent? Do you coach kids? Your local school's parent-teacher organization (PTO, PTA) is undoubtedly looking for volunteers who can enrich the lives of students. Whether or not you have children in that school—or any school—you could share what you know to benefit others. Perhaps what you know is a resource—like a great website. Maybe you have a connection that someone could leverage—to find a job, a volunteer, a mentor, or a sponsor.

Some people get bored with what they have, know, or do. So they move on. Before they've truly mastered one area of their lives, they sidestep into another. Then they get bored and move on again. And they never used their knowledge to help others.

Action is what creates opportunities to expand your knowledge. Don't worry about the things you haven't yet learned. Worry gets you nowhere. Worry is a waste of energy and resources. While you're worrying, you're not taking action.

Think less. Act more. Ask a lot of questions. Answer some of them and research the others. Choose wisely.

And raise your hand.

**❝** *Think less. Act more. Ask a lot of questions. Answer some of them and research the others. Choose wisely. And raise your hand."*

How many times have you been in a classroom or the audience for a presentation or speech and the speaker asks if there are any questions. No one speaks up. Really? If there is an individual knowledgeable enough to stand before a group and impart insights, certainly there is more to learn. Use that opportunity to soak up more for yourself.

Ask "Why?" Why did you get into this field? Why did you make the choices you did? Why did you want to share that with us?

We should all make it our life quest to continuing along a path of learning, but we need to recognize that it's not a race.

# 21 | "Learn from an expert, not a novice—and take the time to learn the difference between the two."

You know those people. You've probably quoted them numerous times.

I'm referring to "They". The faceless, nameless individuals and groups who spout all sorts of knowledge.

*"They say cell phones can cause cancer."*

*"They say no one actually landed on the moon. It was a hoax."*

*"They say we only use ten percent of our brains."*

*"They say you can derail a train by putting a penny on the tracks."*

"They" say a lot of things. It's up to you to decide what to listen to and believe.

One of the problems with the World Wide Web is that there is no filter that alerts you to what you should question. No matter what theory, concept, or belief you want to support, you can probably find sources on the Web to give you that help. The question you need to ask yourself though is "How credible is this source?"

I am careful about where I get my information. I believe you should always seek out an expert—someone who has invested the time and effort in gathering knowledge and filtering out the exaggerations, misstatements, falsehoods, and waste in order to provide a qualified perspective, not just an opinion.

When kids are working on a project or research paper, they'll probably start with a Google search. Then they pick whatever is at the top of the search engine results. It's on the Web, so it must be true, right?

Wrong.

I can post anything I want on the Web. I can write a blog filled with unproven theories and unqualified facts and I guarantee you that some people will believe everything, just because it's on the Web. I can write a review about a book I've never read, a product I've never used, and a restaurant where I've never eaten. I wouldn't do any of these things, of course, but the mere fact that it's possible means we need to be more aware of what we read, believe, and share with others.

We need to teach children to filter. They're quick to question our authority, but not so skeptical about information that comes from total strangers—the aforementioned "They". Teach them not to blindly accept what is written just because it *is* written—even in the news. Explain how human perception can easily alter the truth factor. For instance, bits of information—like quotes from an interview—can be taken out of context. This practice is rampant during political campaigns!

**❝** *We need to teach children to filter. They're quick to question our authority, but not so skeptical about information that comes from total strangers..."*

Snopes.com is a website that confirms or debunks reports, statistics, gossip, and urban myths. Founders David and Barbara Mikkelson launched the site in 1995, when the Internet and the Web were in its infancy, because they recognized the importance of providing a credible source to filter out the truths from the untruths.

FactCheck.org is the site of a nonprofit, non-partisan consumer advocates organization that monitors the factual accuracy of statements made by "political players". The group's goal is to provide voters with a reliable source that will reduce the confusion and deception that faces Americans.

In order for us to be sure that our kids are paying attention to where they find and accept information, we need to do the same. When someone refers to "They", ask for clarification about who "They" are. I'm going to venture a guess here that the speaker doesn't know. And, by asking this question, you at least spark an idea that "They" might not be worth quoting.

Encourage young people to establish credibility in a source for anything BEFORE needing to utilize or rely on it. JFK said, "The time to repair the roof is when the sun is shining." Be careful and diligent in the acquisition of knowledge.

Help your kids to install and maintain a filter in their minds so they can fill their heads with useful, credible knowledge, not hearsay. Teach them how to uncover the experts who can guide them on the right path, and not halt their journey with potholes of misinformation.

# 22 | "You don't drown by falling in the water. You drown by staying there."

When you get into a difficult situation, it's understandable to have a knee-jerk reaction. But some people are so overtaken with such spasms that they can't focus on finding a solution. We call them "worry warts" and "drama queens"—people who are more reactive than proactive.

Sometimes, we get twisted with regard to our situations. We become so tuned into the fact that we have fallen in the water that we don't think clearly about how to get out. We're frantically flailing just to keep our head above water. But what happens is that the energy spent on kicking and splashing is exhausting. The resulting fatigue puts us at greater risk of drowning.

Are you going to allow yourself to drown in two feet of water when the edge of the pool is so near? Will you keep fighting the water in hopes that someone will see and rescue you?

Everyone experiences situations where things don't go as planned. That's called "life". Will you let self-pity define you? Do you allow panic to prevent you from finding a solution? These reactions essentially take your eyes off the ball. You're only able to see where you are, not what you could do to get out.

> *Everyone experiences situations where things don't go as planned. That's called "life".*

Fear can cause panic in a situation. The water is not going to kill you, but your reaction will. If you can relax, you can float, but when fear overrides all reason, you tense up and go under. That fear prevents you from seeing the way out of danger. Sometimes, it's not as difficult as you fear. The shore is closer, the water is shallower, or somehow you can swim farther than you thought possible. But if you stay in one place, splashing and kicking, you're doomed to fail. Look past your predicament. Where do you want to be? How can you get there?

The best way to prevent sinking is to plan for the situation. Careful preparation and practice is the key to safely navigating those dangerous waters. Think about all the fire drills you practiced as a child in school. And every time you take a plane trip, you hear the attendant's speech about what to do in case of emergency. Sure, you stopped paying attention after the second time, but your brain has still absorbed the information. The question is, if there were a fire in your building or your plane started to lose altitude, would you be clear-minded enough to follow the emergency instructions you were given?

Leaders are people who can keep their calm and perform well under pressure. A leader has the clarity of thought to consider the pros and cons of a situation. He makes tough decisions that others cannot make. He puts emotions aside and allows logic to take over. When people are panicking, a good leader can provide the reassurance and direction that guides them from fear to comfort.

This calm decisiveness is something that can and should be taught to children. It's a quality that can be nurtured. To do this effectively, you need to stand back and let your child face those difficult situations and make choices. If you try to resolve every problem for them, you don't give children the opportunity to think through a situation themselves. You create a safety net that isn't all that safe, because they come to rely on you, but you can't always be there to help them out of a tough situation. Don't enable your child to become so dependent on you that they will be unable to realize they can stand up in two feet of water.

We need to nurture people who can lead with confidence and react to whatever comes up. When you cultivate a dependent nature in a child, you prevent them from learning how to thrive on their own. They haven't been allowed to develop decision-making skills. Some people transfer their dependencies from their parents to other people—significant other, boss, co-workers, and friends. Because they don't know how to make the best decisions, how can you trust they will choose the right people to depend on?

Teach children to focus on those things that really matter and let other things go. When a tough challenge hits and they feel like they are sinking, encourage them to stop and take a deep breath. Get over the immediate issue and show them how to place themselves in a position where they can think clearly. Review the available information and show them how to react based on what they know—not perceptions and "what if's". When your children get in a bind, advise them to view the situation in relation to the rest of their life. "How will this affect you a week from now? Six months? Five years?"

Everyone will experience bouts of dealing with the immediacy of what's going on, but beyond a certain point, it's disadvantageous to stay in that reactionary mode. Shift the attention to creating a plan to get out of there. Relax. Look for a way out. Stand up. Focus on solutions and don't let fear sink you.

Bad things happen to everyone. It's how you deal with the tough times that sets you apart from others.

# 23 | "Don't fear life. Step out of your comfort zone once in awhile."

We all have our own comfort zones. We find security in these familiar places. It's a stable foundation that makes us feel safe—a place or activity that is so familiar to us that we don't fear surprises.

School can be like that for children. After they complete a few grades, they move on to another school, like middle or high school. This change makes them nervous because they're stepping out of a comfort zone. Will they know how to find their classes? How are they going to remember a locker combination? What if the teachers are mean?

Moving from one school to another does have some comfort though, because children know their friends will be there on the first day, providing a sense of familiarity. But when they graduate high school and head to college, they're off to a new adventure—and pushed right out of their comfort zone. They have to acclimate to a new environment with new people, new procedures, and the risk that they won't fit in. Freshman year in college is an emotional roller coaster for young people and their parents because they are thrown into a completely different environment.

The same is true when you move to a new home. It's usually exciting for parents, but traumatic for school-age children, who may leave behind everyone and everything they have come to know, only to start all over again.

But change occurs throughout your life. If you sit still and just let life happen, you are wasting a precious gift. People who are open to new experiences are steadily gaining knowledge that can propel them to success and happiness. They try new things that lead them to other new things, and opportunities continue to arise.

> **"** *... change occurs throughout your life. If you sit still and just let life happen, you are wasting a precious gift.* **"**

The boundaries of a comfort zone are established at a young age. Look at the little, picky eaters. My friends tell me stories about how their kids will only eat macaroni and cheese, hot dogs, or spaghetti. They're so frustrated trying to get their kids to step outside their dietary comfort zone. One friend said she tried to make it interesting: adding green food coloring to scrambled eggs to make "Green Eggs and Ham", making fun shapes and initials out of pancake batter, and using toothpicks on small pieces of broccoli.

I'm not a fan of broccoli. I don't hate it, but I certainly will not be the first customer if Big Bob's Broccoli Barn opens up near me. My wife, however, *loves* broccoli. When we got married, guess what we had with dinner every day? To keep the peace, I ate it.

Coconut is a different story. I think people fall on one end of the spectrum when it comes to coconut—love or hate. My wife falls on this latter side. I can't get her to try it. She can't get past her association with the "hairy stuff" on the coconut shell. I think if she ever competed on "Fear Factor" and they told her she had to eat coconut, she'd give up right then and go home.

I brought home a bag of dried coconut for our kids to eat as a snack, rather than cookies or chips. I thought it would be great to try something new. Not only wouldn't my wife try the coconut, but she wouldn't even touch the bag!

Do you remember as a child saying, "I'm not going to eat that stuff. I hate it!" And your parent would answer, "How do you know you don't like it if you don't eat it?"

For all we know, my wife might love coconut, but her mind is preventing her from trying it. She's missing an opportunity to expand her palate and embrace all sorts of other culinary experiences that use coconut.

Your parents were right. You never know what you might like if you don't try.

For me, I hate cold weather. But I thought that skiing might be a way for me to enjoy the winter. I did it a few times. And I discovered that my dislike for being cold far outweighed the fun I had on the ski slopes. I tried. Now I know that I don't want to ski again.

Neale Donald Walsch, author of the "Conversations with God" book series, said, "Life begins at the end of your comfort zone."

It doesn't mean you have to jump out of a plane or give up your worldly possessions. You can take baby steps. Listen to a different type of music or musician that you wouldn't ordinarily choose. Try out a hobby. Join a group or club to meet new people. Even go to a church of a different faith to see what their gatherings are like.

Try unplugging from your technology for a day or a weekend, Turn off the cell phone, the telephone, and everything electronic. Instead, read a book, play a good, old-fashioned board game, visit a nearby place you've been thinking about, plant a garden—anything as long as it connects you with something other than the Internet or a power source.

Step out of your comfort zone and do something good for yourself and others. Volunteer. Mentor. Teach. You'll learn more than you know.

**"** *Step out of your comfort zone and do something good for yourself and others. Volunteer. Mentor. Teach. You'll learn more than you know.* **"**

Consider confronting a fear. If you're afraid of public speaking, join a Toastmasters International group. They're everywhere!

If you're afraid of heights, try going to the top of a skyscraper and stand at the window. Put your hands on the glass. Or start with a climbing wall and work your way up and up and up.

Cecilia Aragon was a fearful child. She couldn't climb a ladder because of her fear of heights. She didn't even get on a bicycle until she was 11 years old. But when she was a grad student at the University of California at Berkeley, she got up the courage to ride in a four-seater airplane. During the flight, her friend encouraged her to take over the controls—and she did. They flew over the Golden Gate Bridge and Aragon says, "I was in heaven. This is my dream. This is it!"

This young woman who broke out in a sweat on a ladder as a child became a stunt pilot and competed in the World Aerobatic Championships. How did she do it?

"I feel the fear," she admitted. "It just that I use it. I use it to make my flying sharper rather than paralyze me."

Like Cecilia Aragon, try taking a risk. Open yourself up to something that makes you uneasy. Be willing and eager to tackle new challenges and opportunities. Your life will fill up with knowledge, experience, and memories, and with each step out of your comfort zone, you will rely less on "the usual" and thrive on "the possible".

> *...with each step out of your comfort zone, you will rely less on "the usual" and thrive on "the possible".*

Then share the wealth with the children in your life. When you see them escape into a comfort zone, coax them out with creative ideas, videos of people doing different activities, photos of interesting places, and books filled with adventure.

Now, I do believe that if you're too open-minded, your brains will fall out, but that applies more to the indecisive than the unadventurous. Open your mind wide enough to welcome opportunities and broaden your world.

# 24 | "Don't live in the United States"

I recently went to a Chinese New Year's celebration. As you might expect, most of the celebrants were Chinese—except me. One African American guy among a scattering of dignitaries and 300 native and foreign-born Chinese Americans.

When I told a few friends that I was going to this event, they asked me why I would want to do that. I guess that's a fair question, since I would be a very small minority. But I was invited by one of the leaders of a Chinese-American business group, and felt it was an honor to be included. Plus, I was really curious.

The evening was enlightening. They started out by playing "The Star Spangled Banner, which I didn't expect at a Chinese New Year celebration. Then they played the Chinese national anthem. The whole night was eye-opening because I got a glimpse into the Chinese culture that I probably couldn't have otherwise, short of going to Beijing. The food was not the usual fare you would be served at a Chinese restaurant, unless you're one of those people who can order in Mandarin and then enjoys the food that the ordinary patrons never experience. I tried everything that was served at this party, eager to immerse myself in the opportunity to step out of my culinary comfort zone.

There was a Chinese-American man sitting at the same table as me. Like me, he spoke no Chinese. He had never been to China. He was so far removed from the cultural foundation of this event that he said he felt like a fish out of water. In fact, he said I fit in better than he did. Maybe there were fewer expectations of me, since I clearly wasn't Chinese. Possibly, the people who understood the meaning of the event wanted to welcome me into their culture, so they made a greater effort to embrace me. Maybe because this was a group of businessmen, we shared that common connection.

Whatever the reason, it was wonderful to get a glimpse into something different from my own view of the world. I like experiencing different cultures and understanding what makes them tick. Opportunities like the Chinese New Year party show me that the global community is coming closer to home, and we have to open our eyes to take it all in. The people who ignore this change are likely to become as extinct as the dinosaurs during the Ice Age.

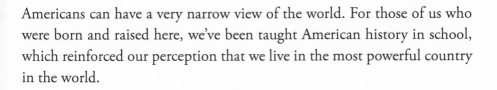

**❝** *... the global community is coming closer to home, and we have to open our eyes to take it all in.* ”

Americans can have a very narrow view of the world. For those of us who were born and raised here, we've been taught American history in school, which reinforced our perception that we live in the most powerful country in the world.

I'm sure that history books in Germany and Japan would have very different presentations of the two World Wars from ours. Does that make them wrong? No, it's all about perspective.

I celebrate national pride, but I don't believe we should let it blind us to the emerging environment of our multicultural community. The face of America is changing. In 2012, almost 758,000 became naturalized citizens, with the majority of them coming from Mexico, the Philippines, India, the Dominican Republic, China, and Cuba.[2] According to the 2010 Census, the Hispanic population in the United States accounts for 16.3 percent of

2    U.S. Naturalizations: 2012, Department of Homeland Security, Office of Immigration Statistics; Annual Flow Report, March 2013; http://www.dhs.gov/sites/default/files/publications/ois_natz_fr_2012.pdf

the total, which is 43 percent more than in 2000. By 2050, it's estimated that about one out of every five Americans will be foreign-born, and these immigrants will constitute 82 percent of our population growth. For the first time in this country's history, whites will comprise less than half of the population—expected to be 47 percent in 2050, as compared to 72.4 percent in 2010.

As our country's population shifts, so will many other things. Many businesses are emerging or growing to capitalize on the growing Hispanic market. Those people who want to lead will have to learn how to embrace different cultures—from their workers to their customers.

We need to change up systems, starting with the schools. Children in China begin to learn English in third grade. Conversely, a Chinese language teacher would have a hard time finding a job in an American public school. Those schools that teach foreign languages usually limit the choices to French and Spanish, and they don't offer that curriculum until middle or high school.

We've got to think more broadly than our personal environment, regardless of where you live. The "melting pot" that used to be limited to the major cities is spilling over to other areas, and new Americans are looking for the same lifestyle changes that native-born citizens enjoy, like rural and suburban living.

A long time ago, we started participating in an interesting Christmas celebration that was sponsored by the Jewish congregations in our community. They invite Christian churches and essentially do Christmas at the synagogue. Everyone involved discovers that the holidays have different meanings, depending on your perspective.

In order to be a leader, you need to take different experiences, beyond your own, and realize the relevance to other people. You have to be able to take the experiences of different people and integrate them into your organization so that it remains current and benefits from the multicultural experience—which will keep you relevant in this changing environment.

When my second daughter was born (14 months after our first), my wife and I decided to give the girls a more unique experience than conventional childcare. We hired an au pair through an international organization. The au pairs come here from their home countries for one year; often, they are young women who are trying to gain experience to further their careers at home, like hospitality and tourism.

We've hired au pairs from Germany, Colombia, South Africa, Poland and Mexico. Our whole family benefits by being exposed to these interesting young people, their cultures, traditions, and languages. We learn to think more broadly, not limited by what's familiar, but getting a more global experience. Our daughters are growing up realizing that there are many countries outside of our own, and they behave, think, communicate, and live differently. Whenever I travel abroad, I always seek out local guides who will introduce me to the local culture and people off the tourist track, so that I can gain a more genuine experience and broaden my perspective on the world.

We need to understand that our way is not the only way. There are things you can do in the U.S. that, if you do it in the Middle East, they'll come running after you. For example, showing the soles of your feet is offensive, so you shouldn't cross your legs when sitting across from a person from this culture.

And here are a few other offenses:

- Using the thumbs-up sign to an Australian, Arab, or Israeli

- Pointing with one finger at a person from a Middle Eastern country

- Giving purple flowers to a Brazilian or Mexican, or lilies to a Chilean, because these flowers are associated with death

- Passing a business card with your left hand to a Chinese person

- Giving books to a native of Hong Kong, because it's considered a curse

- Putting your arm around the shoulder of a Taiwanese person

- Touching the head of an Indian child, because it's considered the seat of the soul

- Talking to a British person with your hands in your pockets

- Flashing the American "OK" hand gesture to a Russian

- Confusing Ukrainians with Russians

There's a saying, "When in Rome, do as the Romans do." That means to follow the culture in the place you're living or visiting. But here in the United States, there is no longer a single right way to do things.

And it's not just other countries that have different attitudes, habits, language, and lifestyles. We have sub-cultures here in the U.S. I remember the first time I had to do business in New York. There I was, a guy from the South, and I wasn't at all used to the pushy way that New Yorkers function. It was rough for me at first, but as I got to know more people there, I realized that's just the way it is. New Englanders are different than Southerners. Texans act very differently from Minnesotans. And people from our country's heartland certainly don't share the same lifestyle as California natives.

If you want a deli sandwich on a long roll, depending on where you are in the U.S., you'd order a sub, grinder, hero, or hoagie. Carbonated beverages are known as soda, pop, or tonic. Same stuff, different names—but all of them are American.

These differences make our country more interesting, as does the influx of people who bring their cultures here.

It's important to understand, especially for young people, that we live in a world of assorted cultures—race, religion, and ethnicity. And these will become valuable lessons as they grow up and enter a diverse workplace. We need to focus in on getting people to open their minds to other cultural experiences.

The point of this Peanut Butter Principle is not to discourage people to live in the U.S., but rather to look at the world as being your hometown, to become knowledgeable and comfortable with other cultures and countries. We don't have a lock on anything here in America. It's a great melting pot, but it's also good to get out and experience the other cultures in the world.

# 25 | "When you're going through hell, keep going."

In May 10, 1940, Winston Churchill assumed his post as Prime Minister of the UK. At the time, the Germans were waging war in Europe. They invaded France, The Netherlands, and Belgium. Two weeks after Churchill took office, British troops were pushed back to the port of Dunkirk, France. The Nazis were closing in. With the German's air and sea power outnumbering them, the British faced almost certain annihilation.

As the Nazis halted briefly, 340,0000 British soldiers were evacuated from Dunkirk. The Nazis then seized control of France.

Churchill was a powerful speaker and he rallied his people not to give up or give in. He vowed that, "we shall never surrender" and told his countrymen, "If you're going through hell, keep going" and "Never, never, never give up."

For 19 months, until the United States entered World War II, Great Britain's Royal Air Force battled the German Luftwaffe. Although outnumbered, the RAF eventually pushed the Nazis out of England. Throughout the ordeal, Churchill continued to build courage, strength, and tenacity in his people so that they wouldn't cave in. He kept the hope alive that they would not just survive, but would emerge victorious. With German planes dropping bombs on his country, Churchill stayed focused on leading his country with conviction that they would not be stuck in this hellish situation for long.

When you feel as low as you can go and you're circling the drain, it's hard to pull yourself up and believe that there's something good up ahead. You might feel that failure is your destiny, but that belief is a self-fulfilling prophecy. You **will** miss 100 percent of the shots you don't take! I know from experience, that if you give up and allow yourself to be in a bad place, then you are the one responsible—not your job, the economy, your spouse, or anyone else you see fit to blame.

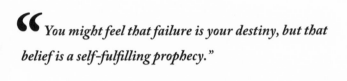

**" *You might feel that failure is your destiny, but that belief is a self-fulfilling prophecy.* "**

In his song, "If You're Going Through Hell", Rodney Atkins says that even "when you feel like there's a sign on your back, says I don't mind if ya kick me" and "things go from bad to worse—you'd think they can't get worse than that, and they do."

Here's the chorus of Atkins' song:

*If you're going through hell,*

*Keep on going, don't slow down.*

*If you're scared, don't show it.*

*You might get out*

*Before the devil even knows you're there.*

If you stop in your tracks, you're stuck there. Think about the "fight or flight" instinct. When something is on fire, you hurry to extinguish the flames. Hose it down. Drop and roll. Block out the oxygen fueling the flames. Toss salt on a grease fire. Whatever it takes, you jump into action to douse that fire and contain the damage.

Keep that same mentality when you feel like the world is pummeling you with bad times. Don't wallow. Don't accept this as your destiny. Grab that hose and fight your way out of the hot spot.

I know that people face all kinds of pain, tragedy, and hardship. The downturn in the economy left tens of thousands of people jobless, homeless, or both. Business closed. The stock market hit record lows. The outlook remained bleak. Good, honest, hard-working people have suffered the consequences as the result of decisions they had no part in making.

In times like these, you can continue to ask, "Why me?" and look for other people to blame, but that doesn't hoist you out of that dark hole you're in.

You can also turn to your faith. If you are a spiritual person, this is the time to rely on that connection with a higher power. I don't just mean that you pray for a solution and then sit and wait for results. Have faith that there's a reason for you being where you are. Rabbi Harold Kushner, author of "When Bad Things Happen to Good People" was inspired to write his classic book when his young son was diagnosed with a deadly disease. He tried to understand why the God he served would take his child. He wrestled with the problem and shares his insights in the book.

"Pain is part of being alive, and we need to learn that," Kushner said. "Pain does not last forever, nor is it necessarily unbearable, and we need to be taught that."

You need to challenge yourself to work through the tough times so that you can experience the reward waiting for you at the other end. The flowers will bloom, but only after the rain.

Just don't allow yourself to drown in that downpour. Churchill said, "Attitude is a little thing that makes a big difference." When we can control our mindset and focus on finding the way out of a bad situation—with a positive attitude—then we empower ourselves to also be in control of our own futures. It's not destiny, but effort that makes the difference.

You can relate this to smaller children by reminding them of the nursery rhyme of "The Itsy Bitsy Spider". The rain washed the spider out of the spout, but then the sun dried up all the rain, and the itsy bitsy spider climbed back up again.

You can only climb out of that dark place when you allow yourself to see the light and find the conviction in your heart to reach for it.

# 26 | "Neither success nor failure is ever permanent."

The earth keeps turning, causing the sun to rise and set. That means every day presents a new beginning. It brings you an opportunity to start over, make changes, and achieve something new. What you do with this gift is up to you, but if you sit back and assume that your yesterdays define today and tomorrow, then they will.

However, if you recognize that life is ever-changing, then you have some work to do. Whether your past is filled with success or riddled with failures, you still have a way to go, and every day is a chance to be better, smarter, happier, and more fulfilled.

People who are content to rest on their laurels will soon find that they are perched on a withering branch that can't support them forever. They keep looking back to what they've done in the past, but with each day, that vision gets farther and farther away, until it disappears.

**❝** *People who are content to rest on their laurels will soon find that they are perched on a withering branch that can't support them..."*

In 1968, artist Andy Warhol coined the phrase, "In the future, everyone will be world-famous for 15 minutes." Think about the news stories that rule the media—local, national, and worldwide. The valor of heroes is celebrated for a short time. A writer, musician, actor, or artist is only as memorable as their current work. "One-hit wonders" fade into the past.

Their books and CDs are in the "bargain" bin at local stores.

Do you remember Los Del Rio? This Latin pop duo formed in 1962, but didn't gain notoriety until its hit single, "Macarena", was released in 1994. It took 32 years to become an "overnight sensation". Although still performing, "Macarena" was Los Del Rio's only hit. However, they did collaborate with another group, The Baha Men. This British reggae band was formed in 1980 and made a hit with "Who Let the Dogs Out" in 2000. They disbanded in 2011, with no other notable recordings.

Do you remember Mark Hamill? If you're a fan of the original Star Wars trilogy, you remember this actor who played Luke Skywalker. Although cast mates Carrie Fisher and Harrison Ford went on to achieve greater acting fame, Hamill's notoriety was even outdone by the movie's non-human performers: C3PO, R2D2, and Chewbacca.

When Buster Douglas entered the boxing ring to battle Mike Tyson for the heavyweight boxing championship in 1990, he was a long shot. The odds were 35 to 1 in favor of "Iron Mike", but Douglas won the fight and the title. He defended his title later that year, and lost to Evander Holyfield—and retired after the fight.

You probably know some people from your past who stood out "back in the day". What have they done since that time? What happened to those people who were voted "Most Likely to Succeed", "Smartest", or "Best Athlete"? Did they live up to their potential? Or are they still reveling somewhere in the memories of yesterday?

Recently, I've run into people who were influential when I was in high school and college, but their development seemed to have stopped back then. Their mental attitude and actions are stuck in the 80s.

Do you want yourself or your child to be someone who lives in the past or thrives in the present? Whatever you achieve—or fail to achieve—use your precious time now to prepare for the next step in your life. Build on your success or overcome the failures. Use your accomplishments as steppingstones and your missteps as valuable lessons learned.

**❝** *Use your accomplishments as steppingstones and your missteps as valuable lessons learned."*

No matter what has happened in your past, there's always the next thing. Even Oprah Winfrey has her "next chapter". She may have retired from her daily television show, but this highly successful woman isn't ready to accept that her ability to achieve can be stuck in neutral.

If you've been successful, build on what you did to get there. Aim for "better". Even someone who is at the top of their game can achieve a personal best. What is yours?

Maybe the next great step in your life is a career change. Most people I know changed their career about three times after college—unless they were solidly on track with professional training, like a doctor, lawyer, accountant, or tradesman. Even some of those professionals have decided to forego their chosen field to pursue something more challenging or fulfilling. When these people made the move to something different, they recognized that their past did not dictate their future. They took control of where they would go and navigated their own route to a new destination.

My father-in-law had been the pastor of one of the largest African American churches on Long Island, New York. He also held an important municipal position. The man was actively living his life and working to make a difference in the lives of others. Even when he was nearly 90 and so-called "retired", he talked constantly about "the next thing" on his list. He never stopped until he passed away, and I have no doubt he is still leading others from his higher place.

It's also important to remember that everybody is going to fail at some point in their lives. Any person who has ever achieved something has also failed, probably more than once, in their lives. I don't know a good leader who hasn't experienced failure. They don't dwell on the mistakes, but learn and become even better, stronger, more effective leaders.

> **"** *...everybody is going to fail at some point in their lives. Any person who has ever achieved something has also failed, probably more than once..."*

It's essential that you share this insight with the children in your life. A young person who experiences setbacks has a smaller frame of reference. What may seem minor to an adult can be debilitating to a youngster. Look at the teenagers who commit suicide. We see their loss as senseless; they saw their lives as hopeless. In the perspective of their short lives, they didn't have the depth or breadth of experience to see that this painful time was just a blip on the radar of a much bigger, fuller life. Instead, they caved in to what they perceived as insurmountable challenges. We will never know what they could have achieved, what differences they could have made in the world around them.

A gas station owner spent nine years developing a recipe for frying chicken in a pressure fryer because it cooked faster than in a pan. "Colonel" Harland Sanders submitted his "secret recipe" 1,009 times before a restaurant accepted it.

Walt Disney was fired from his first job as a cartoonist because the editor said, "he lacked imagination and had no good ideas." Disney started an animation studio in Kansas City, but the business went bankrupt. And it was all up from there.

Comedian Jerry Seinfeld was booed off the stage the first time he did a stand-up act at a comedy club.

After his first acting audition, actor Sidney Poitier was advised by the casting director, "Why don't you stop wasting people's time and go out and become a dishwasher or something?" Instead, he pursued acting and became the first African American to receive an Academy Award for Best Actor (for "Lilies of the Field" in 1963).

Babe Ruth was known as a slugger during his days as a professional baseball player, but he also held the strikeout record (1,330), which lasted from when he retired in 1935 until another slugger, Mickey Mantle, beat it in 1964. In fact, if you look at the list of all-time strikeout leaders, it reads like a Who's Who of baseball stars. What does this tell you? If you want to make a hit, you've got to take a swing.

**❝** *...if you look at the list of all-time strikeout leaders, it reads like a Who's Who of baseball stars. What does this tell you? If you want to make a hit, you've got to take a swing.*"

When asked about his abundance of strikeouts, Ruth said, "Every strike brings me closer to the next home run."

You can't move forward when you're constantly looking back. A happy, successful future belongs to those people who can learn from the past, live fully in the present, and work toward a better future.

PART

# FOUR

## RELATIONSHIPS

While you're helping your child develop his or her "Super Self", don't forget that building and maintaining healthy relationships with other people is also essential. They will have to live, play, work, and deal with people every day. Relating to others runs the gamut of emotions—loving, satisfying, frustrating, challenging, rewarding, combative, and everything in between. When you take the time to help them understand how to successfully interact with others, you also give them the ability to make a positive impact on others—essentially, paying it forward by inspiring people to follow their lead.

It all starts with "Playing well with others", so don't wait to start this part of the life lessons.

# 27 | "Learn to follow, to learn, to lead, and to serve—in that order."

Some people say that great leaders are born. While I believe that certain personality traits can be inherited, I don't believe in natural-born leaders. Leadership skills can and must be cultivated in order to become ingrained and effective in the long-term. As far as I know, scientists have not located a particular gene that is linked to leadership.

If you subscribe to the theory of emotional intelligence—which I do—you recognize that successful leaders share certain EI traits: self-awareness, empathy, self-control, motivation, and social skills. These characteristics distinguish them from managers. Just because you can tell people what to do doesn't make you a good leader. It simply means you're a taskmaster. There's a big difference between managing and leading. Supervising isn't leading. That's herding. Leadership means people follow willingly because they believe in you, not because they are tethered to you in some way. Yes, employees will "obey", but if they don't respect you, they are merely bowing to your will, not supporting your vision.

> **"** *There's a big difference between managing and leading. Supervising isn't leading. That's herding. Leadership means people follow willingly because they believe in you, not because they are tethered to you in some way."*

A person who wants to be a good leader needs to follow a particular progression of learning: learn to follow, to learn, to lead, and then to serve. You can't skip any step in this process. There are no shortcuts. Nor can you jump around.

## Step One: Learn to follow.

You've heard that you have to learn to walk before you can run. The same dynamic holds true for leadership. You can't be a leader without followers, and you can't build a following until you've learned what it takes for one person to choose to follow another.

> **"** ...*you can't build a following until you've learned what it takes for one person to choose to follow another.*"

Allowing yourself to be in a subservient position will give you valuable perspective on the view from this side of the team. What do you see? Is there a leader in front of you who motivates followers, who builds their trust and confidence? What qualities do you want and expect in the person you are going to follow? Watch carefully. Notice how a good leader relates to followers. Learn how an effective leader connects with and responds to the people who rely on him or her to guide them.

As a follower, you learn what to do and what not do in a leadership role. And a good leader will not ask a team to do anything that he wouldn't or hasn't. The leader of a platoon, for example, has worked his way up through the ranks and literally learned in the trenches how to be a good soldier. As a result of this experience, he is respected by his followers.

The television show "Undercover Boss" puts incognito CEOs as workers in their own companies. There, they interact with unwitting employees who don't know they're working side by side with the boss. Week after week, the executive in each episode ends up enlightened by the experience, learning more about his company and the people who make it run. Often, one of the featured employees receives some kind of bonus—like money to pay for childcare, a car, or an education. While those perks are nice for the few employees involved, the true reward is for the entire company, which is run by someone who better understands the needs of the followers.

The next time a youngster whines, "Why do YOU always get to make the decisions?" explain that leadership is a process and they're learning how to follow.

## Step Two: Learn to learn.

What does "learn to learn" even mean? Maybe I should say, learn to *appreciate* learning. A lesson learned isn't one that is merely memorized. Memory fades. True learning comes from first appreciating that you don't know everything, that those who teach are there for a reason. You need to be subservient and respectful to this fact so that you open yourself up to the reality that there is wisdom you need to gain. You don't do that by sitting in a classroom, but by being fully engaged in the lesson.

Young people need to understand that the process of learning is gathering the knowledge, processing its meaning, and applying it to real-world situations.

The fatal flaw I have often witnessed in "wanna-be leaders" is that they are so consumed with the desire to be "in charge" that they fail to incorporate the valuable knowledge and lessons that will make them effective. They are skimming the surface of knowledge because they were in the know-it-all mindset when that wisdom was being presented. They failed to properly process the gift that was given to them.

We have a young generation of people who were raised with a sense of entitlement. They believe that if they graduated with good grades from a prestigious university, then they have paid their dues and are ready to reap the rewards. I wish I had a ladder in my office so that during these job interviews, I could show them where that achievement is situated in the success scale. I respect hard work, but a college degree, to me, is a beginning. It's an investment in the future, not a guarantee.

Teach your children to value the learning process. They should ask questions, pay attention, raise their hands, and do more than memorize their lessons. Encourage them to think about ways they can apply what they're learning to their daily lives. Urge them to build relationships with teachers, to take advantage of the opportunity to learn more from those who are committed to cultivating their knowledge and feeding their curiosity.

**Step Three: Learn to lead.**

Once you have mastered the lessons of learning to follow and learning to learn, you can take the next step and learn how to lead. You know, from being a follower, what matters in this regard. Now you have to integrate these lessons into your leadership education.

I've told you about Emotional Intelligence (EI), which has been shown to be an accurate barometer of forecasting leadership ability. Daniel Goleman, one of the leading EI experts, described the contrast of conventional intelligence and EI.

"Every businessperson knows a story about a highly intelligent, highly skilled executive who was promoted into a leadership position, only to fail at the job. And they also know a story about someone with solid—but not extraordinary—intellectual abilities and technical skills who was promoted into a similar position and then soared. Such anecdotes support the widespread belief that identifying individuals with the 'right stuff' to be leaders is more art than science."[3]

Researchers, like David McClelland, have studied EI and determined that a higher "EQ" contributes to better leadership performance. Goleman reported, "McClelland found that when senior managers had a critical mass of emotional intelligence capabilities, their divisions outperformed yearly earnings goals by 20%. Meanwhile, division leaders without the critical mass underperformed by almost the same amount. McClelland's

[3] Goleman, Daniel, "What Makes a Leader?", *Harvard Business Review On-Point 3790,* January 2004

findings, interestingly, held as true in the company's U.S. divisions as in its divisions in Asia and Europe."[4]

Learning to lead requires ongoing education. There is no finite end, no graduation where you are bestowed the medal of leadership excellence. You must always be alert to the needs of your followers, aware of your own actions, and focused on achieving the group's objectives. Leaders fall from grace every day because they lose sight of the driving vision. Don't ever get complacent about your leadership role. Stay edgy and connected. Show your children that learning is a never-ending quest for excellence. Make them aware of what makes a good leader by showing them examples in their everyday lives—whether that's the principal of the school, a coach, a friend, or a family member making good leadership choices.

**❝** *...be alert to the needs of your followers, aware of your own actions, and focused on achieving the group's objectives."*

## Step Four: Learn to serve.

When their role of leading a group comes to an end, many good leaders retire to a life of serving. Jimmy Carter served one term as the 39th President of the United States (1976-1980). After leaving office, he pursued his passion for serving humanity. Carter worked closely with Habitat for Humanity building affordable houses for people in need. He founded the Carter Presidential Center in 1982 to help struggling countries in Africa and South America establish better health care, promote fair election practices in fledgling democracies, and fight diseases in third world countries. In 2002, Carter was awarded the Nobel Peace Prize in recognition of "his decades of untiring effort to find peaceful solutions to international conflicts, to advance democracy and human rights, and to promote economic and

4    Ibid.

social development."

Jack Welch served as the CEO of General Electric from 1981 to 2001. Under his leadership, GE's value rose 4000 percent.[5] Since his retirement, Welch has been writing and teaching. He is passing on his leadership knowledge to MIT students at the Sloan School of Management and founded the Jack Welch Management Institute at Chancellor University.

Passing on your knowledge is a great way to give back and serve others so that your experience can benefit the next generation of emerging leaders. Parenting is a prime example of leadership. Grand-parenting presents an opportunity for the "retired" parent to impact youngsters from a different perspective—if you can prevent them from just spoiling your kids!

As the leader of your children, help them gain the knowledge they will need to lead others. Guide them through the process of learning to follow, learn, lead, and serve. Model the behaviors you want them to emulate. You will be rewarded when you see that your children step forward and pay it forward so that the leadership trend keeps going and growing.

---

[5]    Jack Welch, "I Fell in Love", CBS News, February 11, 2009.

# 28 | "None of us is as smart as all of us."

This quote comes from management expert Ken Blanchard, co-author of "The One Minute Manager", and I often share it with people who need a reminder of the importance of teamwork. When people work together effectively, they can accomplish so much more than by tackling a challenge alone. It is most often true that two heads are better than one—as long as both heads are focused on the same goal.

I've found in my professional career that neither teamwork nor the team player mentality just happens. That's why sports teams have coaches, orchestras have conductors, and groups need leaders to be successful. Someone needs to be charged with seeing the big picture and steering the group in that direction. The team leader must assess the strengths of the members, recognize weaknesses and gaps, and pull them all together in such a way that they complement one another and achieve the greatest outcomes. A team of highly skilled players, left on their own to come together, will not necessarily become a championship team. If they can't synchronize their skills, it's just a bunch of star players on the field, playing individually and not working with their teammates. They each have their individual role, but don't synchronize with the others.

Think about an orchestra. You could assemble the finest musicians and give them sheet music, but that doesn't guarantee harmony. Each artist plays his or her part as they see fit. Without a conductor listening to the many individual instruments and guiding the musicians throughout the piece, the result could be more noise than music.

Baseball great Casey Stengel got it right when he said, "Gettin' good players is easy. Gettin' 'em to play together is the hard part."

Teamwork begins with the desire for members to give and take, to give their best to the team effort, not for personal gain. For example, if you've ever been to a middle or high school basketball game, you've likely witnessed a ball hog on the court who is totally focused on scoring points. He expects his teammates to constantly feed him the ball because he sees his job as the one who will put up the points and win the game. Meanwhile, the other players don't have the opportunity to hone their skills. They see this one player as the superstar and diminish their own value, submitting to the dominant ball hog. In the end, the "team" is really one player who uses the others in supporting roles—more like minions than teammates. Now, if that player suddenly can't play—injury, poor grades, whatever—what happens to the team? The other players haven't developed their skills sufficiently to make up for the loss of one person in the lineup.

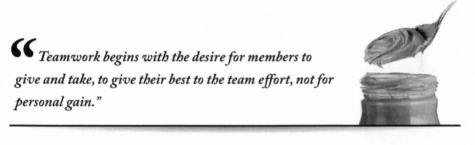

**“** *Teamwork begins with the desire for members to give and take, to give their best to the team effort, not for personal gain.”*

We see this situation in professional sports. In 2011, the Indianapolis Colts' quarterback Peyton Manning was out for a full season, due to a neck injury. Without Manning at the helm, the team—always a top contender—fell apart and had one of the worst seasons in the team's history, winning only two games and losing 14. It was the first time in ten years that the Colts didn't make the playoffs.

What's interesting is that three years before Manning's season on the sidelines, New England Patriots quarterback Tom Brady sustained a season-ending knee injury in the first quarter of the first game of the 2008 season. The loss of Brady, who led the Pats to three Super Bowl championships in four years, prompted many fans to think the season was lost. But back-up quarterback Matt Cassel, who trained closely with Brady, helped the team post a very respectable 11-5 record.

New England cultivated a system of teamwork. Coach Bill Belichick developed players to play more than one role. A kicker, for example, ran for a touchdown. Defensive players learned offensive moves so they would be equipped with the skills to contribute points to the score, not just prevent the other team from doing so.

A good leader knows how to create balance in a team. He puts people into the roles that suit them, that challenge them, and give the group the chance to achieve better success. He doesn't rely on just one individual, but actively builds everyone on the team to reach their potential and, therefore, contribute the most to the group. By making each member better, stronger, and more experienced, the team benefits. When the team benefits, so do the individuals.

There can be incredible power that comes from working in teams. When I see a group prepare to brainstorm with just a few people—usually management—I encourage them to bring in others who can offer a different perspective. Include the person who answers the phone and has the most direct contact with customers or vendors. Bring in someone who works on the line, handles shipping, does data entry, or some other task. You never know where a great idea will come from, but I can guarantee you that if you rely on managers for out-of-the-box thinking, well, don't hold your breath. A good leader recognizes that a strong team is made up of a broad range of skilled people, so don't limit the possibilities by narrowing your vision.

In Rachel Brady's novel, "Final Approach", one character points out, "When you're problem solving with a team and somebody has an idea, separate the idea from the person talking, because once in a while, a jackass might come up with something useful."

Getting successful results from a team also requires communication—both from the leader and the group's members. Everyone needs to understand the goals. They should also be clear on expectations and guidelines. Make sure everyone is on track with the core values so that they don't overstep the boundaries. For example, you could tell the team you want to find a way to bring back past customers who have drifted away. But you also have to be clear on whom they should contact, what they can offer, and, more importantly, what they **can't**.

Thanks to technology, the workplace is populated by more people than ever who are working with flexible schedules and sharing jobs, as well as working from home or other offsite locations. All of these situations present challenges. You're still the member of a team, whether you're physically present or not. Communication is critical in these situations. It's easy to blame the person who's not there or to make assumptions that someone else is covering for you, but that's a recipe for disaster.

A good leader knows how to create and maintain a culture of teamwork. As in all instances, you start by setting a positive example, establishing values of authenticity and accountability. You recognize effort in your members as well as their achievement, individually and as a group. You help them develop problem-solving skill by letting them find solutions, rather than giving up the answers too freely. Even when you need to step in and mediate problems, you should guide the disputing teammates to find the solution themselves. You don't let an ugly situation linger, because you know that if you let things fester among one or two people, the whole team will become infected. They slip into an unhealthy, negative mindset, and productivity suffers. When people waste time looking for scapegoats and pointing fingers, they aren't moving forward, but falling behind.

Just like the cliché, "There is no 'I' in 'T-E-A-M'", these concepts are important to share with children from the time they are very young. Participating in team sports and scouting are great ways to start them off and teach them how to be a part of a larger group.

A family is also a team. When you create a goal to be accomplished by your family, you can also teach your child the importance of teamwork. Give the child a role in the project. Be sure to explain why this job is important to the "team". Give them "chore" to do around the house.. Without everyone doing their part—no matter how small the job might seem—the team will suffer and the goal won't be realized.

We are relying on a generation of team players who can work together to make sense of the world around them. Get them started now so we don't have a world full of ball hogs!

# 29 | "A leader will have an answer before anyone else understands the question."

If you want to lead, put your body and mind in the front position. You need to be prepared for contingencies because you have the forethought to expect the unexpected.

A good leader is a quick thinker. He can look at a problem, assimilate the conditions, consider possible solutions, estimate the outcome, and then act. And he does this faster and more effectively than the people around him.

What does all this mean? Well, a person who leads others is in a position where he must be a good decision-maker, because people are counting on his judgment. He usually juggles multiple situations simultaneously, so he doesn't have the luxury of sitting and pondering. He has earned the leadership position, based on past successes, but doesn't sit back and expect others to follow in the future just because of what he achieved in the past. He has proven that he can see through a wall of chaos and create a vision of what could be on the other side. And he skillfully makes decisions and takes actions to keep moving toward a goal. Sometimes, that means pulling others along—guiding and explaining to them so they can share the vision. He has to anticipate the next step—the next several steps, in fact—so that he either avoids a possible problem or develops a solution before the followers even see what's ahead.

I recently hired a new assistant. She now has the unenviable position of trying to learn to think like me. She doesn't have to like the way I think, but she has to be in tune with it. Her job requires her to anticipate what I am going to say, need, and do. If I have to ask, then she's not doing her job according to the description she accepted when I hired her.

I've had assistants in the past who were nice, intelligent, and accomplished, but the most important factor in their success was their ability to use their knowledge and wisdom to constantly think on their feet, to come to a conclusion and move on to the next thing. They didn't overthink a situation. What I truly appreciated about each person was that they were decision-makers and action-takers. They delegated as necessary and handled a lot of issues without ever involving me, which made them leaders themselves. So, regardless of your position, you can lead through your proactive mindset.

There are lots of ways to help children develop their strategic thinking. Play games that help them to think a few steps ahead of the next move. Mancala, tic-tac-toe, and checkers are great for preschoolers. From there, move on to Connect Four, chess, and backgammon. Risk is a timeless classic for building strategic thought. Rush Hour and Jenga present puzzling challenges that also teach kids that every move has a consequence. Even Scrabble and Words With Friends require players to work the board. Before playing their tiles, they need to think ahead to what their opponent might do with available double- or triple-letter or word plays that you're leaving on the board.

Game-playing is a fun way to help children look at a situation and come up with a solution. The more you guide young players through making forward-thinking moves, the stronger their strategic planning ability. And you're having fun at the same time!

# 30 | "Not every question warrants an answer."

There are some questions that should be answered immediately, like "Do these pants make my butt look big?" Don't hesitate. Just say "No."

There are other questions that should be carefully pondered before answering, such as "Do you have any idea what you did?" Trust me, you only get two tries at getting this one right.

Then there are questions that don't need an answer. Like those that are asked to lead you into a conversation you'd just as soon avoid. And the ones that the person asking already knows the answer to, but wants to see if you're as knowledgeable or enlightened. And then there are the questions that come from laziness—the asker wants you to do the thinking.

I don't answer all questions. People might think that's rude or arrogant, and I don't mean it that way. I politely look at them and say, "I just don't have an answer for that."

Sometimes not having an answer is a wise answer. Proverbs 17:28 states,

"Even a fool who keeps silent is considered wise;

when he closes his lips, he is deemed intelligent." When you're asked a question that isn't well thought out, does it deserve a thoughtful answer? I don't care what anyone says. There IS such a thing as a stupid question!

For example, Tina worked in the order department of a publishing company based in the United States. Let me add that she had a college degree in psychology from a state university, so she was not without an education. She asked her supervisor, "I have an order that's going to England. Do I send it by air or truck?"

Her supervisor responded, "How big are the tires on the truck?"

An even more learned (allegedly) lawyer asked a witness in a court case, "Doctor, how many autopsies have you performed on dead people?"

The physician replied, "All my autopsies are performed on dead people."

Because he was required to do so, the doctor answered the question. In another circumstance, he likely wouldn't have bothered.

Maybe the question you choose not to answer is inappropriate. Someone is nosy, curious, and doesn't respect boundaries. Well, just because that individual has the nerve to ask you a personal question, doesn't mean you have to give an answer. I had a co-worker who was always probing into my personal life. She asked me questions about things that I don't even discuss with my friends, let alone someone I work with. On several occasions, I simply told her, "You really don't need to know that", but she didn't get it. So, she kept asking, but it was my choice not to answer her questions.

Other questions that don't warrant a response are born of laziness. Think of all the times someone asked you how to spell something because they didn't want to look it up. This is made even worse when that someone is sitting in front of a computer that contains just about any answer you could possibly need!

When I look at social media—like Facebook and Twitter—I see so many people wrapped up in discussions about things so meaningless that I won't even take the time to read their posts, let alone add my own opinion. I frankly don't care what celebrities are doing, unless it impacts my life. I don't care about some foolish statement that was reported in the news. I filter out the junk so it's not taking up valuable bandwidth in my brain that could be invested in something that really matters.

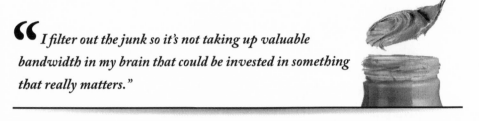

> **"** *I filter out the junk so it's not taking up valuable bandwidth in my brain that could be invested in something that really matters."*

To quote a Bible verse, "Foolish and unlearned questions avoid." If someone is trying to engage you in a pointless discussion or argument, walk away. Your time is too precious to be wasted on meaningless chatter.

I'm often asked for an opinion—at work, at home, by friends, even by the news media. Honestly, sometimes I really don't have an opinion. This movie or that movie, this restaurant or that restaurant—just pick one, because I truly, from the bottom of my heart and soul, don't have any preference. Yes, it drives my wife crazy, but I tell her that I would rather defer to her when I don't have an opinion than conjure up something that isn't real.

There are people who are such ardent proponents of certain causes that they don't hear what anyone else has to say. They're perched up on their soapboxes, preaching to the world—regardless of whether or not someone is listening. Even if you're in agreement, you will not be heard.

I focus on the things that matter and avoid those that don't. Many things that enter into our environment are inconsequential to our success or failure. It's just noise. You can choose to let it distract you or tune it out.

I don't know everything, but I don't have a desire to know everything. I want to expand my knowledge on the topics I care about. I don't worry about keeping up with current trends, unless they're relevant to my life.

Along the same lines, I'm not impressed with "star power". If a celebrity is an achiever, then I will study that person to see how they achieved the things they did. Our actions are what make us superstars. Somebody who is famous without achieving anything—like so many reality show "stars" and trust-fund babies—aren't worth discussion. An individual's personal life—particularly difficulties and failures—don't interest me either.

A small child might ask you repeatedly, "Why?" It's like a game of verbal ping pong. For every response you give, the child asks, "Why?" Finally, out of exasperation, you might pull out the old faithful of parental answers, the trump to any child's challenge:

"Because I said so."

That's not a good answer. It's just a response.

Kids are curious by nature. They're going to ask a lot of questions. You should certainly support their growing minds. At the same time, it wouldn't hurt to instill in them the importance of filtering so that they can decide when they should ask or answer certain questions. If you fail to do so, you might get a call from the school someday when your little angel tells an entire classroom about what Mommy and Daddy said last night!

ERIC FRANKLIN | 147

# 31 | "There is a difference between a decision and a commitment."

It's easy to make a decision—well, for some people. But let's be clear that making a decision is not the same as making a commitment.

A decision is more like a promise. You decide to quit smoking. You decide to lose weight. You decide it's time to settle down.

Any of these decisions can be reversed. You simply change your mind.

Think about all the times you decided to take on a project. "This weekend, I'm going to paint that room!"

At the time you made this declaration, you fully intended to follow through. Then the weekend rolled around. You slept in late on Saturday. You went to the home improvement store, got distracted by all the other "bright and shiny" objects in the store, did a few other errands, and returned home. By that time, it was too late to get started. So, you decided to do it the following Saturday.

Then you got invited to go out with friends—brunch, golfing, shopping… whatever. You decided you could simply put off the painting project for another week. After all, the room is not going anywhere, right?

So, although you **decided** it was time to paint that room, you weren't **committed** to actually doing the job.

It's easy to change your mind. We do it every day, for a variety of reasons. Sometimes, like painting the room, that decision was just something you kind of wanted to do—not following through wasn't going to hurt anyone, so no big deal, right?

Maybe. Maybe not.

When you make a decision that involves other people, they might not see your choice as flexible as you do. If you tell your kids you've decided to take them to Disney World and then change your mind, they'll be devastated. To them, you've made a *commitment* to take this vacation together. To you, it was just a really great idea.

If you decide to help your friend move and then change your mind, you've damaged the trust that person has placed in your word. Your friend saw your decision as a *commitment* to help.

I recently heard Dr. Leonard Smith discuss the difference between decision and commitment. He illustrated that a pilot makes a decision to fly a plane. He gets into the cockpit, goes through the pre-flight checklist, and prepares for take-off. He can, of course, change his mind, get up, and leave the plane; however, once he is barreling down the runway and ascending into the air, he has committed to flying that plane. He can't go back on his decision without creating significant problems. If he were to walk out of the cockpit at that time, while the plane is soaring, it's going to come crashing down.

The reverend also cited the example of Japanese gymnast Shun Fujimoto. In the 1976 Summer Olympics in Montreal, the 26 year-old Fujimoto was competing for the team gymnastics medal. During the floor exercise, he broke his knee cap. Fujimoto knew that if he withdrew, his team had no chance of winning the gold medal. Not wanting to let down his teammates, he kept his injury a secret and continued to compete.

He was in such pain, he said he wanted to run away, but he continued. He scored a 9.5 (out of 10) on the pommel horse, where his knee problem didn't impede much on his performance. Then Fujimoto performed on the rings, with his knee well braced. His routine was stellar. He completed a triple somersault twist dismount from eight feet above the mat and landed squarely on his feet, avoiding any penalty on the landing, even though he completely dislocated his knee with this dismount. Still, Fujimoto held his stance long enough and then crumbled to the floor in agony. He scored a 9.7—his personal best—and the Japanese team won the gold medal by just four one-hundredths of a point, the narrowest margin in Olympic gymnastics history.

When asked how he was able to perform so well with such excruciating pain, Fujimoto replied, "My desire to win was greater than my moment of pain."

Fujimoto didn't just decide to compete in the Olympics. He was committed to winning. He was committed to his team, his sport, his country, and his personal goal.

"It's hard to beat a committed individual," Dr. Smith says, adding, "We live in a world where commitment seems to be the exception and not the rule. We don't want to commit. People are willing to make a half-hearted contribution, but rarely a wholehearted commitment. They opt into a cause, but don't commit to it. People are committed to not being committed."

**❝** *People are committed to not being committed."*

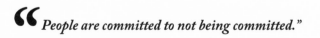

I see it all around. Parents won't commit to helping out at their children's schools. Parent-teacher groups (e.g., PTA, PTO) are always begging for volunteers—some of whom make a promise, but then don't follow through. They don't want to be responsible to show up, required to participate, or otherwise obligated. Why? Because they value their time so much that they won't commit it. It's like a miser grasping tightly to pennies.

Some people will announce their decision to do something, like it's a done-deal. "I'm going to lose 30 pounds!" "I'm going to run a marathon!" "I'm going to go back to school and get my degree!"

Their friends and family congratulate them for this decision. They're looking to the future and envisioning the accomplishment, as though making the choice is the same as the achievement. Everyone celebrates a statement. However, there's no action with it—just words.

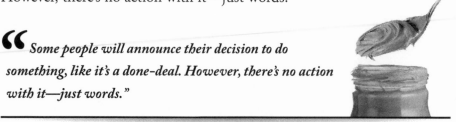

**❝** *Some people will announce their decision to do something, like it's a done-deal. However, there's no action with it—just words."*

I have to ask these people, "So how are you going to do it? When are you going to start? What's your timeline look like?"

In other words, put your money where your mouth is. Show me how committed you are to your words.

A member of the board of Jazz at Lincoln Center pledged $327,000 to the organization and then reneged on the promise. The group saw the gift as a commitment and had probably earmarked those funds for a specific use. They sued their own board member to fulfill the pledge.

There may be valid reasons for a change of heart, but you need to understand how your decision to "re-decide" affects others. A decision is merely a declaration of intent. Anyone can do that. If my wife asks me where I want to go to dinner, I can say that I want Italian food and we head out the door. There, I've made a decision—with no action involved whatsoever.

Or I can decide not to decide and let her make the choice. But it doesn't mean I'm committed to having a particular meal at a particular restaurant. We can get all the way to the restaurant and I can make yet another decision that I would rather go elsewhere. Sure, my wife is going to be mad when I tell her I want to change our destination as we're about to walk in the door. So, I can *decide* if I would rather incur her wrath by telling her, "You know what? I've changed my mind", or choose to keep my mouth shut and just keep walking into the restaurant.

A decision is a choice. It's a promise to do something. Commitment is demonstrated by action and results.

**" *A decision is a choice. It's a promise to do something. Commitment is demonstrated by action and results.* "**

Try to explain the difference to your child. Give them examples of decisions (promises) and commitment (action). More importantly, be sure they know that only commitment delivers results, and only the results you deliver will define who you are.

# 32 | "A position is granted. Influence is earned."

It starts innocently enough. A youngster comes to you, overflowing with enthusiasm, and asks permission for something.

"Can I go to the mall with Chris?"

"Can my friend sleep over?"

"Can I stay up an hour later?"

"Do I have to be home in time for dinner?"

For whatever reason—you don't want your kid hanging around the mall, your evening plans don't include having another child in the house, you know your youngster needs sleep, dinner time is family time—you say, "No."

Of course, your child pushes.

"Why not?"

You try to reason, but, clearly, you're not getting through to the child. Then you throw out that parental trump card that is meant to end all discussion.

"Because I said so."

You probably cringe when you say it, because you remember how it felt when your mom or dad tossed that line at you—frustrated and dissatisfied. The answer was a "non-answer" because it gave no rationale behind the decision. "Because I said so" conveys, "I'm the boss and you must obey. Period."

This fairly common answer reflects the family hierarchy—a sort of class system—where the parents are the bosses and the children should respect their authority. But you've certainly met parents who were not what you would consider worthy of their child's respect. I don't think respect is a birthright. We all know that becoming a parent is a biological occurrence, but *being* a parent is a day-to-day job that requires a whole toolbox of skills.

Becoming a parent is a position that you're granted, just like being hired for a job. You come by it, by choice or happenstance. You might be hired to be the boss, but that doesn't mean you're automatically going to be respected. You're given the authority to make decisions on behalf of your group, but what you do with the leadership opportunity will determine whether or not you gain respect. If you step into a position and repeatedly make the wrong decisions, you won't cultivate the respect you need to lead the group.

And it's a two-way street. You may have people in your life who say they *deserve* your respect. Some do, but not everyone. Just showing up doesn't command respect. Just because you've been raised to believe you can do no wrong doesn't automatically grant you the honor of respect.

Respect is earned, not given. You can't simply wave a title in front of people and expect them to bestow respect on you. They might *obey*, but that's not the same. People will do things begrudgingly when commanded—and when something is done this way, I guarantee that it's not done with the utmost care, attention, and pride. I've learned that when you respect other people enough to give them clear answers and direction, they will accord you respect in return. They still might disagree with your choices, but will respect that you are in charge and that it is their job to follow.

Those people who are good at decision-making and managing people will be the ones in charge, no matter where you are or what industry you're in. When you're good at getting results, you will rise to the top. A good leader will move an entire organization to achieve more. A good leader respects the gifts and talents that people have and leverages those attributes to move the whole group forward faster and higher. A smart leader doesn't try to shape team members into a clone of himself, but sees the unique contribution that diverse skills, experience, and perspective bring to a team.

Someone suggested to me, "You need to duplicate yourself and your business would be better."

I replied, "We don't need another 'me'. What I need is for people to maximize their capabilities and for everybody to achieve. I've hired these people for their unique skills. Trying to get a person to squeeze a square peg into a round hole is not what we're trying to do. That would make this company really one-dimensional and that would hold us back."

John Thain, former CEO of Merrill Lynch, is an example of a bad leader who lost respect. Although the company had lost billions of dollars, Thain asked the board for a $10 million year-end bonus in 2008, with the rationale that he had prevented further losses. It was soon discovered that the executive, who was earning about $83 million per year, had used $1.22 million in corporate funds to renovate his office, two conference rooms, and a reception area, including $1,100 for a trash can. He resigned that position soon after this news was made public.

Look at leaders like Adolf Hitler, Saddam Hussein, Josef Stalin, Pol Pot, Louis XIV, and Kim Jung III. They led with fear, which is bullying, not leadership. Their people didn't respect these leaders; they submitted to them for fear of their lives.

The Institute of Executive Development conducted a leadership study and found that 40 percent of new leaders fail within the first 18 months. A similar study by Human Capital Adviser estimates that number to be considerably higher, with a 60 percent failure rate.[6] The most common reason is the lack of interpersonal skills and goal conflicts. They didn't communicate well with their teams and, like John Thain, served their own needs, not those of the majority.

So, how can you teach a child the meaning and value of respect? You can start as you would with any other lesson: by example. Cast out the "Because I said so" card from your deck. Take the time to communicate with a child with respect. Explain your criteria for making a decision, and teach a child to develop the same. Just as any good leader would do when presented with a request, ask, "Why do you think this is a good idea?" Encourage them to make decisions with more thought and less impetuousness. Teach them the importance of understanding consequences. When you build better communication, you establish a foundation on which you can build respect. You hear them out, give them the opportunity to present their case, and consider their position. You might end up right where you started—saying "No"—but at least you respectfully listened and considered the argument in favor of a "Yes" answer. And who knows? You might even be persuaded to change your mind.

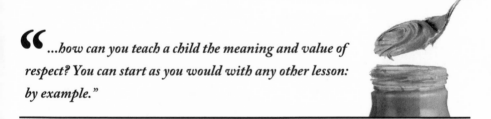

**❝** *...how can you teach a child the meaning and value of respect? You can start as you would with any other lesson: by example."*

One of the worst situations you can create with your child is for them to assume that you're "just gonna say 'no' anyway". So, they either don't bother coming to you or sneak around. When they do that, they could be making bad decisions that you don't even know about. When you can talk through differences together, you build respect, trust, and faith in one another.

---

6    "Young Leaders and Failure", HumanCapitalAdviser.com, March 9, 2012; http://humancapitaladviser.com/?p=1096

# 33

## "Use your words carefully."

I admit that my bluntness can, at times, come across as insensitive. I'm not a callous man, but I'm not always careful with my word choices—or maybe my timing. Any way, I came into the office one day and a woman who had been out for a couple of days with a back problem had returned to work. I saw her talking with her supervisor, so I went over to welcome her back. I asked her how she was feeling. Nice enough, right? She answered, "I'm doing okay."

Then, I said, "Are you sure? 'Because you don't look that good."

I said this out of concern. She looked to me like she was still in pain. I thought that maybe she should go home and rest some more. I thought I was being an empathetic boss, but her supervisor looked at me and scolded, "That's not nice!"

The woman with the back pain shrugged it off and added, "You know Eric and how direct he can be."

I was startled. I really thought I was being a good guy. Not only was I admonished for saying something blunt and offensive, but I also discovered that I'm apparently a repeat offender!

We need to be more careful when choosing words. We all know that words can hurt. We tend to remember insults and complaints much longer than the compliments, because they make a deeper impression.

Some young people believe they can say anything to anybody. There are no filters.

One woman was telling me that a friend came to her home with her 13 year-old son. He looked at this woman's wedding portrait and said, "No offense, but you didn't look that great in that picture." She was dumbfounded, and her friend was mortified. She said to me, "This was my wedding picture. That was the best I've ever looked and this kid was telling me I didn't look very good."

I asked her how she responded. She told him, "Well, since you told me 'no offense', I know you didn't mean to offend me, but I'm going to be equally honest with you and tell you that I'm hurt by what you said."

"I didn't mean to," he said, looking surprised at her and also catching the "if looks could kill" glare from his mother.

"Well, here's a little advice. Just because something pops up in here," she said, tapping his head, "doesn't mean it has to come out here." She pinched his upper and lower lips together.

Someone recently told me that she feels she can say anything to her mother, because they're best friends. While I applaud this type of close and open relationship, there are still plenty of things that I would never say to my parents, because some of it may be inappropriate. Just because you want to say something, doesn't mean your mother wants to hear it! Language is two-way communication and we need to realize how our words are being heard and processed.

You might think, "Well, if this person is a friend, they'll listen to whatever I have to say." Maybe you define a friend as someone who will accept you no matter what you do or say. That's not a friend; it's a pet. A friend should be there to listen to you, but also to make you a better person. Iron sharpens iron. Whether from a friend or parent, you need someone who will give you constructive feedback because they care about you. A friend is someone who will tell you when you're wrong, from a place of love and compassion. They will tell you the truth when you need to know it, even when it's hard to hear. Only really insecure people need to surround themselves with "Yes men" who affirm their every thought.

I've seen people with truly horrendous singing voices audition on "American Idol". A huge audience is cringing as these people embarrass themselves. When a judge asks, "Who told you that you can sing?" they usually say, "My friends and family." If you cared about someone, would you let them experience such public humiliation?

We also need to be more respectful of language, in general. Proper grammar and spelling have fallen prey to cultural "advances". The advent of texting has added even more damage to our language. I wonder how many young people think that "rele" is the correct spelling for "really".

The spell-check feature in word processing programs, like Microsoft Word, isn't foolproof, but too many people assume it to be. If you typed the word "wit", for example, when you intended to write "with", spell-check doesn't catch the error, because "wit" is an actual word. And if you think a single letter can't change the entire meaning of a sentence, tell that to the person who sent out a press release announcing that the company was preparing to make a public offering, but left the "l" out of the word "public"!

Emails have converted what used to be voice communication (phone calls, voicemail) into written messages. This shift has exposed a massive problem. Many people who can speak English well can't write it. How many emails a day do you get with errors in them? From typos to run-on sentences to just plain, bad grammar, email messages expose weak English skills, in even the most learned people. I know plenty of executives and professionals whose emails would earn them an "F" from a high school English teacher.

And hip-hop music has taken plenty of liberties with the English language. This genre has tremendous impact on young people, who may not realize that phrases like "ain't got no", "don't got to", or "I seen" contain horrifically bad grammar.

Worse yet, they don't care.

We need to impress on young people the importance of using good English. Even an intelligent person can come across as stupid when they use poor language skills. While slang might be cool right now, remind them that they will not always be hanging out with kids their own age who all speak the same language. They will need to influence others—in college and job interviews, when making a presentation, writing a report, or going for a promotion.

One of the best ways to improve English skills is to read often. When you read with a young child, talk about certain words and what they mean— both in the literal definition and the meaning in the story. Encourage them to find new words and learn how to use them. Give them examples of good and bad grammar. Play word games, like Scrabble, Words With Friends, Wild Word Garden, Hangman, Balderdash Junior, Bananagrams, and crossword puzzles.

Teach them to pay more attention to their language—from possibly hurtful or rude comments to slang to wrong usage. People won't necessarily commend when you use language correctly, but they most certainly notice when you get it wrong!

**❝** *People won't necessarily commend when you use language correctly, but they most certainly notice when you get it wrong!"*

# 34 | "Your accomplishments should speak for themselves. Don't interrupt."

Have you ever met someone who feels a need to recite his resume during the conversation? He talks about where he went to college, the places where he has worked, the recognition he has achieved, and probably some of the impressive people he knows. These same people will give you the same spiel the next time you meet, too.

The thing is, I'm not impressed. I think a person who has to bring so much attention to his accomplishments either hasn't achieved anything truly significant or worthwhile, or is terribly insecure and in need of affirmation.

I ask myself "Why?" Why aren't they comfortable with who they are? Why do they need to tell everyone what they've done? Shouldn't those accomplishments they offer up so frequently have enough merit to satisfy these people?

Someone who constantly harps on their college years when he's 30, 40, or 50, clearly hasn't done much since then. Now, I have just as much pride and love for my undergrad alma mater, Hampton University, as the next guy and I acknowledge the valuable experiences and top-notch education I received there 30 years ago, but I focus on what I'm doing now and planning to do tomorrow.

Warren Buffett, one of the most influential and sharpest financial minds today, graduated from the University of Nebraska. He was denied acceptance to Harvard Business School. Oprah Winfrey went to Tennessee

State University. "The Simpsons" creator Matt Groenig graduated from Evergreen State College, a school with no grading system or required classes. Award-winning actor and director Ben Affleck attended Occidental College, but dropped out. Larry Ellison co-founded Oracle software after dropping out of the University of Chicago. Astronaut John Glenn attended Muskingum College, but never graduated. In spite of that, he became the first man to orbit the earth and, later, a United States Senator. Their individual achievements are reflections of their efforts, not where they went to school, or even if they did.

I went to a banquet recently and after dinner was served, the emcee delivered a lengthy introduction of the keynote speaker. He went through a long list of credentials so that we would know why we should pay attention to this presenter. I would have much preferred that time to be given to the speaker. I know that such introductions are customary, but do they really need to drag on? Is it intended as a tribute to the speaker? Does the speaker want that tribute?

Well, one of the reasons I endured the rubber chicken dinner was because I knew of this speaker's reputation and accomplishments. I already knew who he was and wanted to hear him speak. I believe most, if not all, of the other people in the room shared my feeling. So, we didn't need this recitation to get fired up. If anything, it splashed some water on the flames. Like Renee Zellwegger's now-famous line from the movie, "Jerry Maquire", "You had me at 'hello'."

In contrast, at the 2013 Academy Award ceremony, host Seth McFarlane gave the following introduction for Meryl Streep: "Our next presenter needs no introduction."

And with that, he walked off the stage and Streep emerged.

McFarlane was 100 percent right. No one in the audience needed to hear a litany of this heralded actress' achievements. If you don't know who Meryl Streep is, you probably wouldn't be watching the show any way.

I've delivered many speeches and presentations. If I need to bring up my experience or achievements as supporting fact, to lend credibility to what I'm saying, then I mention them in my speech. If I can't convince you of my point without reciting my resume, then I'm not effective at what I'm trying to deliver. The only purpose of a resume is to get you in the door. Once you've stepped in, tuck it in your pocket. You can't live on your resume once you've got your job.

> **❝** *The only purpose of a resume is to get you in the door. Once you've stepped in, tuck it in your pocket. You can't live on your resume once you've got your job.* **❞**

The most effective people let their achievements do the talking for them. They do what they do for the results, not the accolades. They've built a reputation and earned such respect that people will speak for them, as opposed to that person having to repeat all the things he did in his life.

So, how do we teach our kids that bragging isn't a good quality? I think it's more about instilling confidence in them so that they soak up the value of their accomplishments, like a sponge. Bragging is like squeezing all that achievement out of the sponge and leaving it dry.

Certainly, we want to build self-confidence in children, but there's a fine line between curbing boastful behavior and nurturing self-esteem and confidence. As youngsters, they don't yet have the ability to recognize boasting. They know that "Look at me, Mommy" gets them the attention they want. They're seeking praise, and you should deliver it.

But when a child holds such achievements over others, it becomes boastful. Instead of "Look what I did", they're saying, "I can do that better than you."

Rather than scold the boastful child, suggest that they teach the other person how to master the skill they're so proud of. Teach them that the value of a talent is not in boasting about it, but in sharing it with others.

**❝** *Teach them that the value of a talent is not in boasting about it, but in sharing it with others.* ❞

Bullying often results when kids don't understand this point. When a child feels superior over another, she bullies others so she can stay perched on that self-constructed pedestal. Maybe she knows she's pretty or a great athlete, and looks down at those who don't measure up in her eyes. Some children bolster their superiority with things they had nothing to do with, like their parents' financial status. They brag about their nice house, the new cars, the expensive vacation, and all the gadgets their parents have bought them. They strut around in expensive clothes and show disdain to any child who hasn't had the benefit of such indulgence.

No child should fall victim to a class system. They are developing people, finding their way in a tough world. The family you are born into is the luck of the draw. A child has no control, no choice here. It's what they do with their own lives that truly matters. The way in which they create themselves using what's available—seizing opportunities—will define them as adults. They should put their energy into becoming a good citizen of the world and not diminishing others.

Good or bad, successful or not, a person's life is going to speak for itself. Don't interrupt. Anyone who has to stand up and blow his own horn is surely hitting a sour note.

# 35 | "Only dance with those who are already on the floor."

I like to dance, but that doesn't mean I always want to. Sometimes, I'm just not in the mood. And no amount of pleading, cajoling, whining, or tugging is going to get me out of my chair. Okay, perhaps a scornful eye from my wife, but that's about it.

This is where my advice comes from. If you want something, choose from your available options. Pick something from the menu. Don't expend energy trying to get what isn't there, change what won't be fixed, or, worse yet, reinventing the wheel. Sure, I always welcome a challenge, but I also choose to invest my time, energy, and resources in endeavors that will make a positive difference—in my life and the lives of people around me. I set immediate goals that are achievable. And if there's someone or something right there in front of me—on the dance floor—then I know the likelihood that this person wants to dance is far greater than the sullen-faced woman off in a corner with her back to the floor. If that person has chosen to situate herself so far from the dance floor, I guarantee you that she isn't interested in taking part.

Why spend your valuable time trying to convert someone? Instead, invest the time improving yourself, and not trying to shape someone else into what you want them to be. Maybe you need to take an inward look and see if you're the one who needs improving. Possibly you need to be more tolerant of someone's foibles or open to hearing other opinions. Remember the "it's not you, it's me" excuse that people use to reduce the pain of rejection? Well, maybe it *is* you!

Take people for what they are, not what you think they should become. Who says you have the perfect vision any way? The unique traits of other people give us a wealth of diversity. If everyone fit into your vision of the ideal individual—the ideal mate, friend, parent, sibling, co-worker, employee... whatever—you would be living in a "Stepford" world. You would rob yourself of discovering interesting people and exploring opportunities that broaden your world. Spending too much time trying to change someone else just slows down your own progress.

I've heard it said that men choose women with the hopes that they stay exactly as they are. Women choose men figuring they can change them. In any relationship, you can't shape someone to fit you—intimate, friend, whatever. Take people for what they are and improve yourself, first and foremost.

Accept differences and learn from them. Appreciate that a different approach than your own has merit. Use the strengths of others to complement your weaknesses, and vice versa.

This is also a valuable lesson for leaders. Any good sales manager or marketing director knows that it's easier and less costly to retain your customers than to go out and convert prospects. Those companies and organizations that invest in maintaining their clients and members through user-friendly policies and exceptional service demonstrate that they value those people who choose to be among their network. A leader who is so busy cultivating new followers that he ignores the people who are already committed to him is not effectively serving them. Some businesses institute policies that punish their customers. Banks are a good example. They lure you in with the promise of free checking and then charge you to use a teller! Stores with unforgiving return policies will lose shoppers. Part of Blockbuster's demise was the high rental and late fees. When Netflix and Redbox came along with more customer-friendly policies, Blockbuster busted.

Apple became a global brand, in part, because of its amazing innovation. Gadgets like the iPod, iPhone, and iPad have attracted consumers who never bought into the company's Mac, but the company's service—brilliance like the Genius Bar—treats every Apple user like a valued customer. Even when people can buy less expensive competitor versions of their beloved smartphones, mp3 players, and tablets, they turn to Apple, because they know they will be taken care of.

When you, as a leader, tend to the needs the people who are loyal, you naturally cultivate a greater following.

PART

# FIVE

## GOOD CHOICES

How many people have you known who were good at decision-making? And how many of them made good choices?

There's a difference.

The ability to make a decision is key to your child's success. Indecision means your child will miss opportunities—which are then seized by the more decisive thinkers.

Making good choices means that your child is not only decisive, but also thoughtful about the consequences of those decisions.

When your kids are young, you're there to guide them through this process, to help them weigh their options and make the choices that are best for them. But as they grow into adulthood, you won't have that kind of influence. Invest your time now in teaching them how to consider their choices and to then be decisive in picking one.

# 36 "There's nothing wrong with showing your emotions. Just set them aside long enough to make good choices."

In William Styron's book, "Sophie's Choice", the title character is a Polish-Catholic mother during the Nazi takeover in her country. As she is being taken to a concentration camp, she is forced by a Nazi officer to choose between her young son and daughter. She can only save one; the other will be killed.

Meryl Streep played Sophie in the film version and she poignantly portrayed the woman's agony in making the choice.

I don't think I've ever seen a situation with a more difficult decision, a more powerful demonstration of emotional control. The book's title has become synonymous with choosing from a no-win set of options.

I've often had to deal with tough choices. We've all been there. The tougher the situation, the more emotions are involved. So, it's absolutely essential that we teach kids how to rein in their emotions when needed.

I'm not proposing we raise a generation of androids. Sure, a poker face comes in handy when you don't want to tip your hand, but people who never show emotion create a barrier between themselves and the people around them. Leadership requires a connection with followers. You can't create or maintain that relationship when people see you as cold, calculating, and unresponsive.

Still, there's a time and place to succumb to your emotions—and it's not in the heat of a confrontation or when you're on the verge of making an important decision. If you've ever had to deal with a screaming, pleading, whining, or foot-stomping child, you know that the emotion creates a barrier to communicating. How many times have you said (or heard), "When you calm down, we can talk about this"?

When you're trying to get what you want—whether it's closing a big business deal or gaining control of the remote—you most definitely get the upper hand in negotiating the deal when you can contain your emotions. You tackle the situation with logic and a rational manner.

I've been doing a lot of reading lately about emotional intelligence and its impact on leadership. People who have knowledge can only go so far; those with high emotional intelligence have proven to surpass them, time and time again.

One of the key traits of a strong emotional intelligence quotient (known as "EQ") is self-control. The ability to remain calm when all others lose their cool enables you to reduce the chaos to a manageable level. In the past year, we have seen some horrible tragedies: the killing of 26 innocent children and adults at Sandy Hook Elementary, the bombings at the Boston Marathon, the Washington Navy Yard shooting, and the tornadoes that ripped through Oklahoma. In every tragic instant, leaders emerged. With the horror raining down, first responders kept focused on providing care to the victims and a sense of security to all of them and the communities involved.

At Sandy Hook, music teacher Maryrose Kristopik huddled her students in a closet and tried to speak calmly with the elementary students while the gunman banged at the classroom door. Teacher Kaitlin Roig barricaded her 15 students in a bathroom and told the kids, "There are bad guys out there now. We need to wait for the good guys."

Moments after the bombs exploded at the 2013 Boston Marathon's finish line, first responders who were in the nearby medical tent ran towards the explosion to help the victims, rather than seek protective cover. Their quick action certainly saved lives.

In Oklahoma, residents lined up to help in the rescue of schoolchildren buried in the debris of an elementary school flattened by the titanic tornado. They contained their emotions, working silently so that rescuers could hear voices of children still trapped.

In every instance, government officials—from the local FEMA and police to the governors and the President—came out to guide everyone through the aftermath. Of course, they felt deep emotion at the senseless loss of lives, but they could not lead others if they became unraveled.

Wiping away a tear or getting choked up when addressing a crowd is acceptable in these situations, but turning into a blubbering mess doesn't exude confidence. Followers need to believe that their leader is emotionally above them. They rely on the individual to make wise decisions, not emotional ones. Look at King Solomon's decree. When two parents claimed the same child, he declared the baby should be cut in half and divided between the two adults. The woman who cried that she couldn't allow the conflict to kill the child was then judged by Solomon as the true mother, because she was the one who would give up her own child in order to save his life. And now the name "Solomon" is synonymous with wisdom.

Could the king have made a call like this if he allowed his emotions to jump in? Certainly, he had no intention of harming the child, but he managed the self-control necessary to get the job done here.

We all face tough decisions at many points in our lives. In some cases, the choice comes between what you know to be right and what your heart tells you to do. Let me tell you that feelings change as time and situations change. You have to look beyond the immediate because that becomes history almost instantly. Take the time to ponder over the long-term consequences. And do it without allowing emotions to color your thinking.

Since I'm on the subject of emotional self-control, I have to add another category of perpetrator here: Those folks who create their own storms and then get upset when it rains. They bring chaos with them like leading a dog on a leash. And they seem to thrive on that craziness! You know these people. They don't just enter a room; they burst in, carrying with them all of their tribulations. "Oh, the traffic was insane!" "I can't believe how long it took me just to get a cup of coffee!" "I have to tell you what just happened to me!"

These are the Sonic Boomers. Their outbursts are the epitome of uncontrolled emotions. They are so self-absorbed that they don't see how they impact the people around them. From a minor interruption to a major upset, their volcanic emotional eruptions do nothing productive.

In fact, any time you lose control of your emotions, you become unproductive. I think emotions should be like a faucet. You turn it on and off when you need water. You don't leave the water running, because it's a waste—and you'll probably flood the place. Turn it on, get what you need from it, and turn it off. And, yeah, it *should* be that simple.

**❝** *... emotions should be like a faucet. You turn it on and off when you need water. You don't leave the water running..."*

# 37 | "A lesson not learned will be repeated."

"Fool me once, shame on you. Fool me twice, shame on me."

It's one thing to be gullible or naïve. That's an innocent or trusting nature. It's another to be ignorant—and by that, I don't mean "stupid", but someone who "ignores" what's happening in the world.

Some ignorant people make the same mistake over and over. They repeatedly choose the wrong people to have a relationship with—whether a friend or significant other. They ignore product reviews and buy things that have been known to fail. And no matter how many times they get themselves into trouble for bringing up a sore subject with the wrong person, they keep doing it. Every single time, they get the angry index finger wagged in their face with the scolding of "Will you never learn?" or "How many times do I have to tell you?", but it all just flies right past their head, never absorbed into their memory.

Albert Einstein defined insanity as the act of doing the same thing over and over again, and expecting a different result.

So, those people who don't learn from their mistakes are not just ignorant, but insane as well!

If you tell a child not to touch the stove because it's hot, you trust (okay, you hope) that she listens to you. Well, she very well might not, but she'll learn pretty fast if she goes ahead and touches that hot stove! And I guarantee, she will not do it again.

Yet, you go to a restaurant and a server brings a dish, carrying it with a potholder, and says, "Be careful. This plate is very hot!"—but you touch the plate any way.

"Oooh, that's hot!"

A child is naïve. The person touching the hot plate is ignorant.

We know that fire is hot, snow is cold, and ice is slippery. Most people also know that all-wheel drive and all-weather tires will not help you when you're speeding on a snow-covered or icy road. But every winter, ignorant drivers prove that they haven't adequately learned to respect road conditions and cause accidents. And what do they say then? "I had no idea the road was so slippery."

The snow and ice should have been a good clue.

My dad says, "Eventually, you have to go back and figure out how every choice worked out for you."

When you don't take the time to go back and assess the impact of your choices, you risk repeating the bad ones. When an experiment succeeds or fails, the scientist goes back to analyze what contributed to or caused the outcome. Like Edison, who went back thousands of times to find the right filament material for a light bulb, you should learn from the things that have gone wrong in your life—by accident, by purposeful choice, or by someone else's hand. Valuable lessons are in there. Ask yourself each time, "What did I learn from this?" Put that insight on a mental post-it and tuck it away—not too far though—where you can remind yourself later and avoid repeating the situation.

I do believe in giving second chances though. When I go to a restaurant and have a bad experience—the food was bad, the service was slow—I could just leave and vow never to return. But I know that things happen.

The server or chef could be having a bad night. If I base my opinion on this one experience, I might be robbing myself of a great meal at that place in the future. So, I speak to the hostess or manager and explain why I am dissatisfied. If they actually show that they care about my problem and keeping me as a patron, I will probably come back. If I get a shallow apology, I realize that management isn't interested in fixing the problem, so the issue will recur. In either instance, I will share the story with other people, who might pass it on. So, my one experience at this restaurant then has a snowball effect. If I was happy and I share it with others, they might try out the restaurant. If they have an equally good meal there, they pass the word. But if I tell everyone I know that the restaurant was terrible, think about all of these missed opportunities for the restaurant.

We all know people who make the same mistake over and over. An individual's development as a happy and productive person (what that means to them) can be arrested by the same hole they seem to keep falling into. This has little to do with how intelligent or sincere a person is. Some of us have not connected with the concept of cause and effect. Others can see the train that's on a collision course with you a mile away, but every time the train wreck happens, you're the last to know it. It is very important that we teach children consistently and from a very early age, that every action has a consequence.

# 38 | "Everything happens for a reason, but sometimes, the reason is you're stupid, and you make poor decisions."

Whenever I say this, I get a confused look, like the person I'm addressing isn't sure he heard me right.

I do believe that things happen for a reason. It's usually not apparent at the point when you're trying to make sense of a situation. Discovering that reason can often take a long time. Meanwhile, we're mired in the muck, wondering when the skies will open up, the clouds will part, and that enlightenment will shine down.

We have to work through a tangled mess and emerge on the other side. And, at last, the reason is exposed. We were meant to leave that job or relationship or home because something, someone, or some place much better was lying in wait in the future, and, had you not left when you did, you wouldn't have been open to this new opportunity. It can be really comforting to believe that there is a happy ending to reward you for surviving a challenging time in your life.

But there are plenty of times when we're not trotting down the yellow brick road on our way to a better, brighter future. We trip up and something unfortunate results. In these cases, the reason things have gone wrong is our own fault. Yes, I'm saying "we", because I'm not innocent here. When I get it wrong, I say, "I messed up on that one." It's not only pointless to steer the blame elsewhere, but it's also counter-productive. How can I ask people to follow me if I turn them out for my own failings? I believe a good leader is one who owns up to his mistakes. If you aren't accepting responsibility, you're placing it in the wrong place, and that impacts your followers.

Author and leadership expert John C. Maxwell observed that "A man must be big enough to admit his mistakes, smart enough to profit from them, and strong enough to correct them."

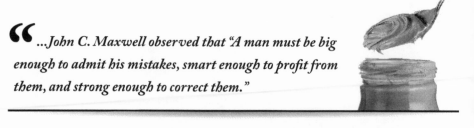

**❝** *...John C. Maxwell observed that "A man must be big enough to admit his mistakes, smart enough to profit from them, and strong enough to correct them."*

Everyone makes bad decisions in their lives. It's inevitable. Some of the consequences of those choices are more serious or lasting than others. It doesn't matter. When you make a mistake, admit it. Somewhere inside, you know that you were wrong and it will lighten your mind to just state that. Even if no one was wronged, admit it to yourself. Don't go looking for a scapegoat. How many times have you heard someone say, "The stupid alarm didn't wake me up" or "The dog ate my homework" (or something like it). Let's be honest here, the job of the alarm is to make a noise, not reach over and shove you out of bed. If you forgot to set the alarm or did it incorrectly, it's your fault, not the inanimate object's mistake. And if you left your homework where the family pet could grab the appetizing papers, then you should have been careful where you placed important things. Dogs do what dogs do.

Then there are those car accidents caused because someone wasn't paying attention. "The car came out of nowhere." "I only took my eyes off the road for a second." Well, when you're the one behind the wheel of a vehicle that can cause a fatal accident, you have to always watch where you're going and what's coming at you. I don't profess to be a flawless driver, but I know enough to double-check before I make a move that involves other cars or objects in my path.

A lot of times, we attribute things that happen in our lives to other people. It's somebody else's fault, we had nothing to do with it. I know that people go through interpersonal issues, marriage and relationship problems, and I never take to heart what one person says about the other during those conflicts. There's culpability on both sides. Even when you think you've done nothing wrong, the mere fact that you ignored the symptoms or failed to communicate better is worth acknowledging. When you're not willing to look at yourself critically, that's a prescription **for failure**.

**"** *When you're not willing to look at yourself critically, that's a prescription for failure."*

You can say something was just meant to be, or shrug it off as saying that it happened for a reason, but that can be an easy out. Maybe you just chose wrong or you did something that was uncharacteristic of you. It happens. That's part of being human. But you need to acknowledge your culpability and then learn from the experience. Change the way you make choices. Be more mindful of the consequences before you decide. Learn from it—both the lesson from the mistake and the act of owning up to it.

Playwright Oscar Wilde said, "Experience is the name everyone gives to their mistakes."

A friend of mine was telling me that she made a fabric doll that resembled her young son—baseball hat, glasses, and all—and she made a small slingshot to put in the doll's back pocket. She gave it to him and said, "Here's your new friend. His name is 'Not-Me'."

Her son looked at her, confused.

"I named him that so when I ask you 'Who made this mess?', and you answer, 'Not me', then I'll know who's to blame."

She said they talked about accepting blame and being honest enough to admit when you've made a mistake. She told him that it's better to do that and then fix the problem than to "waste your brain and mine" trying to figure out who you can blame.

A few times, this mom found Not-Me at the scene of a spill or where something was broken. When she asked her son if he was trying to blame the doll, the little boy said, "No, he was just trying to tell you 'I'm sorry'."

We don't become wiser without stumbling. Life is a lot of trial and error. If you want to grow, you have to take risks. Some will pan out, but many won't. If you waste time looking for people to blame, you're missing the lesson. It's okay to be stupid once in awhile, as long as you don't make a habit of it.

**❝** *We don't become wiser without stumbling. Life is a lot of trial and error.* ❞

# 39 "It's the store's job to sell you stuff you don't need. It's not your job to buy it."

All the marketing, advertising, and hype that hit you square in the face every day is designed to whet your appetite and open up your wallet. It's bait. From the coolest new gadgets to the hottest styles, retailers and manufacturers are doing their best to get you to part with your hard-earned money.

Kids are the easiest targets. They're gullible—easily drawn in by splash, sparkle, and coolness factors. From $80 jeans and $200 sneakers to the ever-growing list of electronics—everything from a $50 video game to a smartphone, laptop, iPod, tablet, or gaming system. If their friends have it, they "need" it.

Plus, kids seem to have more money than previous generations. We saved to get what we wanted. They just ask. Why is that?? Maybe it's the parents who are the gullible ones.

We need to explain to children that everything in a store is there for one purpose: to be sold. The retailers don't care who hands over the cash (or, more likely, the plastic). A store is real estate. Every square foot is laid out for making the most money in that space. That's why they put kids' cereals down low where youngsters can grab it, and then plead with their mom to "please. please, please" buy this four-dollar box of sweetness. The makers of those temptations pay extra fees per store, per month, (tens of thousands of dollars) to get that space on the shelf. It's like renting a shop on Main Street. You pay more because you're getting a prime location.

To sell you more stuff, more often, retailers do what they call "merchandising." They use eye-tracking software that shows them what shoppers look at and for how long, in any given aisle in the store. Then they move the inventory around to make sure it is located where the shoppers are looking.

Retailers entice you with rewards and loyalty card programs to "pay you back" for your spending. Meanwhile, they track your buying habits—what you purchase, how much, when, and how often—so they can dangle enticements to buy more, more, more. They get your mobile phone number and email so they can send you more reasons to buy. They get you to download their mobile apps so you can shop (i.e., spend) anywhere. And, of course, there's always the discount—lowest price of the season, biggest sale of the year…until next week.

I don't blame retailers. It's their job to sell you stuff. It's not your job to buy it. Because of all the opportunities to buy—in and out of the brick-and-mortar stores—consumers have to be smarter. We must recognize that retailers do not make offers out of concern for our needs, but for their bottom line profitability. We have to be more discerning about purchasing, not falling into the trap of special pricing, limited time offers, and one of my personal pet peeves: the free gift. When do we *pay* for a gift? Doesn't the term "gift" inherently imply "free"? It's a bonus, not a gift, and somewhere along the line, you're paying for it. Maybe you pay for shipping or the price of the initial product or service is inflated to cover the cost.

**" *We must recognize that retailers do not make offers out of concern for our needs, but for their bottom line profitability.*"**

Then we have shopping frenzies, like Black Friday, which has now overlapped on a family holiday. People are leaving the Thanksgiving dinner table—or not showing up at all—in order to stand in line, in the cold and sometimes overnight, just so they can potentially get a great deal on a television or computer. Really? Have we gotten so trained by the retail industry that precious family time is sold for a few hundred bucks?

I know women who are slaves to shoes. They buy a pair or two every week—and I'm not talking Payless, but designer brands with designer price tags. OK, you're successful enough to be able to *afford* this guilty pleasure, but you're really an addict. You don't *need* more shoes. You buy things just for the sport of buying and shopping. How many times are you going to wear all those shoes? What's the cost per wearing?

Avid shoppers go into debt because of the adrenaline rush of going out and "hunting and gathering" the latest gadgets, styles, and temptations. Their closets are chock full—whether that's clothing or the industrial size package of paper towels. It doesn't matter.

Now, I admit that I'm a gadget guy, but you'll never catch me standing in a line to buy *anything*—not when I can get it online a few days later, and with free shipping!

If you've been paying attention, Apple tends to use their loyalists as guinea pigs. They have them test out the newest product and then release a new version a short time later, based on their feedback. When they launched the first iPhone, the first adopters spent about $800 to be among this elite group of shoppers. A few months later, after receiving push-back on the iPhone's high cost, Apple lowered the price. All those early buyers who were so eager to get in on the new technology paid the full amount and later, all they got for their loyalty was a $100 credit to spend more money at the Apple Store. When it comes to new technology, I choose to wait, read the user reviews, and simply order mine online, with free shipping. Just standing in line to get something, how does that profit you?

I also don't do Black Friday. I don't rush out to buy the latest release of anything. And I will never catch the midnight showing of the latest alleged blockbuster.

All you have is time. You should devote it to something worthwhile, not sitting in a parking lot all night or walking out on a family event.

We need focus in our perspective, to avoid jumping around from one stimulus to another and prevent wasting time and money on stuff that will lose its luster in a very short time. Go through your closets, garage, and attic and look at what you've accumulated. Think about the cost of doing so. What could you have done better with the money you spent and the time that was essentially wasted on shopping for things you don't really need?

Leaders are not slaves to advertising or hype. They make measured, informed decisions, not impulsive ones. They are not influenced by promises, enticements, or the pressure of their peers. Leaders set the pace and the trends that others follow. In order to be a leader, you have to sometimes go against the tide, against what's popular. If you spend or invest your money the way everyone else does, you're average, going with the flow with everyone else, and sometimes paddling away like crazy just to keep up with the mounting pile of debt.

You've got to be able to look about you and act at the time in the way you need, not give in to some desire to jump the gun before everyone else does. If implementing something before others benefits you in real terms, then that's when you need to do it.

Help your children to understand the difference between "need" and "want". Ask them how an item will change their life. And what will that change look like a month from now? Six months? A year? Encourage them to think beyond the present moment, past the instance of impassioned desire. Look at the big picture and learn how to work toward a larger goal, like saving for a car or a college education. Preserve your wealth for those things you really need.

# 40 | "If what you drive to the bank costs more money than you have in the bank, you're poor."

There's nothing wrong with having things. We all have possessions we want, need, or both. The trouble arises when we put an undue emphasis on the items and the acquiring of these things. Purchasing becomes a habit that is not driven by rational need, but compulsion and other unhealthy motives. We lose perspective—and probably waste money.

Rather than revel in short-term gratification, we need to look at the cost of maintaining what we buy, over the life of the item. A house, for example, might look like a great deal, but it can become a bottomless money pit if the construction or maintenance wasn't done correctly. Remember that you **do** get what you pay forI wrote earlier about my lifelong desire for a Lamborghini. When faced with the reality that I could afford to purchase the luxury car, I decided that paying $4,000 for an oil change just didn't make fiscal sense for me.

My wife has a. . . (excuse me—several) fur coat that she loves, and it comes in handy during the cold winters here in the North. But the price of buying the coat is compounded by the annual storage cost. I've discovered that if a fur is not properly stored and cared for, there will be expensive repair. Lesson learned.

I see people who shop beyond their means. They live in an apartment because they don't have the financial means to buy a home, but then they go out and buy an expensive luxury car. I don't have a problem with renting and this lifestyle makes total sense for some people. But if you don't own real estate because you can't afford it or your credit is a mess, and you go out and buy a luxury car, you're woefully short-sighted.

I don't know if it these people splurge for show or as a way of treating themselves to something luxurious, but, either way, the purchase is frivolous. And I guarantee that these buyers don't limit themselves to one frivolous expense. Maybe they pay $100 for a pair of jeans, show up at a dinner party with a $60 bottle of wine, or feel the need to outfit their precious pooch in designer clothing. I have to ask myself, what's the real return on this investment? In the long run, how will it make a difference in your life? Would the money have been more useful if saved or wisely invested?

Why would you purchase something at a higher interest rate than you would make at the bank—or even the same amount? When you buy a $25,000 car, you pay finance charges (unless you get zero percent). That vehicle is no longer costing $25,000, but $30,000. Is it worth it? The car depreciates as soon as you drive it away, but you continue to pay for it as though it were brand new, with no miles on the odometer. So, you've diverted resources (the down payment and monthly payments) from other investments that could build wealth. Of course, you need a car, but could you purchase something less expensive? What's wrong with a quality, pre-owned vehicle? If you shop around, you can find some great values.

If you're buying a car so that it impresses others, ask yourself this: Does anyone really care what you drive? There's a nouveau riche guy who bought a used Bentley for $200,000 after selling his business (along with purchasing a massive house on the water, several jet skis, and other fun stuff). Do you know what most people said behind his back? "He could have done something so much more worthwhile with that money", "What a waste of money", and "Who is he trying to impress?"

For the people who do care about showy possessions, do their opinions really matter to you? If so, why? Again, think about their values, your values, and the long-term value of spending to impress.

While I'm on the subject of excess spending, let me say that I think credit is evil. We've seen what it does to people. They get into such deep debt that they lose their home, car, worldly possessions, and then file bankruptcy—which punishes their debtors who extended them credit because the individual has lived beyond his or her means and can't repay what he owes to them.

Some people believe they're managing their debt by paying the minimum amount due. They're actually condemning themselves to a life sentence of payments, because the minimum only chips away at interest and finance charges, not the principal. It's like trying to douse a brush fire with a water pistol.

Lenders grant credit like tossing out candy. It's a sweet enticement for the cardholder to go out and buy something they can't afford to pay for at the time. They think credit is good. It's not. This system of "buy now, pay later" enables people to shop without paying attention to the long-term consequence of mounting debt.

I learned this lesson the hard way. I had a mountain of student loans to repay when I graduated college. Then some lenders threw credit cards my way, and I managed to max out my credit limits. I was able to pay the minimum with a "little extra", but when I decided I wanted to buy a house, mortgage lenders told me I didn't qualify for a loan because my debt-to-income ratio was too high.

I took on a second job, tending bar at night. I paid off all of my school loans and credit cards and finally bought my first house. The exhilarating freedom I felt when I unburdened myself of that debt load was something I haven't experienced since. I promised myself I would never get in that financially distraught situation again.

Leap ahead a decade or so. If I had not gotten my debt under control, I would have never been able to venture out and start my own business.

Most of what you need, you can save for and buy yourself. If you are about to hand over a credit card to pay for something, add 20 percent to the purchase price to reflect the finance charge. Then ask yourself if the purchase is still worthwhile.

**❝ *Most of what you need, you can save for and buy yourself.*❞**

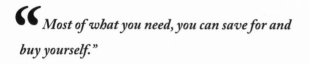

I have gone through some tough times in business, but I was able to come through because I wasn't saddled with debt.

We need to look at how much we're burdening young people with debt when they get out of school. They are starting their professional lives with the weight of student loans. At the same time, they are used to instant gratification. The buying power of a credit card is a license to shop carelessly. Once the consumer builds up a balance, the sinister credit card companies then increase credit limits, adding more fuel to the wildfire. These young people either crumble under the weight of their debt or choose to ignore it.

Meanwhile, their credit rating tumbles—something that seems unimportant when you're 21, but can deal a life-altering blow just a few years later. Employers can look at a candidate's credit score and gain enough information to change the hiring decision. If you show heavy debt with poor payment habits, your behavior shows carelessness, a trait that most employers will not embrace.

We need to empower children from a young age with an accurate understanding that "wealth" is not what you believe you can "afford" but what you can actually pay for—and certainly not with a credit card. Driving a fancy car doesn't make you wealthy. Wearing expensive designer clothes doesn't signify financial well-being. These are items that come and go.

> **"** ... *"wealth" is not what you believe you can "afford" but what you can actually pay for..."*

I knew a pastor who served two parishes in New Orleans. He was a wealthy man, both spiritually and fiscally. Then Hurricane Katrina destroyed both churches, his home, and his cars. He had to start all over again. In an instant, everything he owned was gone. I learned from him and this experience that you can't put value in those things that can be taken away from you.

> **"** ... *you can't put value in those things that can be taken away from you."*

While I'm on my soapbox, allow me to make this point, Bankruptcy is one of the worse testaments of your character. Period.

Certain types of bankruptcy allow you to "reset the clock" of your personal debt—effectively erasing the debt you owe. The problem is that, somewhere along the line, someone gave you access to credit to give you the ability to purchase items that you didn't have cash for.

My friend, Sue, told me that when her home caught fire, she first rescued her 12 year-old son and two dogs. She went back in to get her computer. She returned a third time to gather up photos, which, of course, were displayed all over the place. As her son stood in the front yard, being restrained by strangers, Sue rushed back in one more time, holding a wet towel over her mouth, and looked around her smoke-filled home. She said she ran around in circles, trying to decide what really mattered. In the end, she left with just some clothes for her son.

"I saw a house filled with things and memories," she told me recently. "I will always have memories. Life is what matters."

Fortunately, the fire was contained and the losses were minimal. Sue says she learned not to become too tied to possessions

I don't want my life to be defined by purchases, nor do I want the value of my work to go to useless debt. I love the freedom of financial security, and I share the importance of this feeling with all who will listen. I try to teach my kids that the way they manage money is a testament to their character. When you are responsible with money, you will act similarly with other tasks. When you handle your credit wisely, repaying your debt on time, you prove that you are true to your word. Such responsible and reliable behavior is critical to developing today's young people into tomorrow's leaders. That's some advice you can take to the bank, just not in a Bentley.

# 41 | "Everything you buy is something you have to take care of."

In 1996, Disney timed the release of its live-action version of its animated classic, "101 Dalmatians" during the Christmas holiday season. Viewers became so enamored of the adorable pups in the movie that they rushed out and bought puppies for themselves, even gifting the dogs at Christmas.

Less than a year later, Dalmatians became the most abandoned and abused breed in the United States[7]. One rescue group in North Miami took in 130 unwanted Dalmatians, and said that kind of sad milestone would ordinarily take more than two and a half years to reach. Two counties in south Florida reported that their shelters experienced a 35 percent rise in abandoned Dalmatians after "101 Dalmatians" started the short-lived fad.

As it turned out, the dogs in the movie were not an accurate depiction of this breed. Dalmatians require a lot of exercise and training. They can be aggressive, stubborn, and high strung. In other words, it's not always the best choice for a family pet.

The same thing happened to chihuahuas after the release of "Beverly Hills Chihuahua". And it's not just dogs either. After "Babe" made pigs so irresistibly adorable, people ran out to adopt one. I don't think they expected these piglets to talk like the one in the movie, but they sure weren't prepared to care for a little porker. Before long, animal shelters were taking in former pets that were either abandoned or surrendered.

At Easter time, people get the clever idea they should buy bunnies and chicks—the live ones, not the marshmallow or chocolate version. They

[7] "101 Abandoned Dalmatians", sfgate.com, September 15, 1997

overlook the reality that not only will these cute little creatures grow up, but they also need to be cared for. A few weeks before Easter, I saw an ad in the paper asking people *not* to give in to the urge to buy their own Easter bunny or chick, because so many are abandoned, neglected, or abused when the initial fascination wears off—which is about the same duration as the Easter candy.

Everything you purchase comes with some sort of maintenance. A pet is a commitment—from a couple of years for the small ones like mice and hamsters to 50 years or longer for a parrot. Training and walking a dog or changing a cat's litterbox doesn't deter impulsive buyers in search of a cuddly critter, but those tasks quickly wear on a person who isn't ready for the long-term commitment that comes with having a pet.

Even non-living purchases need care. A car requires maintenance. Clothing needs to be laundered, and that "dry clean only" label will end up costing you more than the purchase price of the item. Then there are the collectibles that look so appealing in the store but soon become nothing more than a dust collector.

A friend was telling me her sister bought her a live orchid for her mantle and a drinking fountain for her cats. Both items require regular care. The orchid came with instructions for watering, feeding, and exposure to light. And the fountain was accompanied with a lengthy manual, a filter to be changed regularly, a tank to be refilled about twice a day, and the need for dismantling and cleaning the many parts every week.

"They were very nice thoughts," she told me, "but I would never, ever have bought either one. My cats are happy with a water dish and I am a notorious plant-killer because I don't remember to water them."

A businessperson looks at return on investment before spending money. What will a purchase give back to you? In some cases, you invest in equipment, because it will save time or lower manufacturing costs. The purchase will essentially pay for itself.

Some business "investments" are made in people. An employer pays the costs associated with hiring, training, paying, and keeping valued employees, including perks like insurance, paid vacations, tuition reimbursement, and other expenditures designed to cultivate loyalty and retention. It costs less in the long run to invest in an employee who has proven to be valuable than to replace him or her, because of the lost time during the hiring and training process, and the uncertainty of the newcomer's contribution to the organization.

The wise spender looks beyond the purchase and considers affordability, which is a combination of purchase and upkeep. Look at the decision from the standpoint of obligating yourself long-term. What will it take to maximize the value of your investment? How much time, money, and effort will be required to take care of this purchase in the long run—and is all that worth it to you?

**❝** *The wise spender looks beyond the purchase and considers affordability, which is a combination of purchase and upkeep.* ❞

Kids always want something, usually for the immediate gratification. They don't see past the "I want". They have to be taught there is a consequence for everything you do—like those poor Dalmatians!

Those people who ignore the consequences are not leaders. They will trip and fall over their bad buying choices time and time again. "Buyer's remorse" will lead them to wasted time, money, and resources. They will miss out on opportunities, fail to appreciate what's important, and not commit to the care and maintenance that is essential to everything from purchases to relationships.

It's easy to say "yes" when a child is pleading with you, but if you want to cultivate good decision-making, self-control, and smart money management skills in your child, don't do what's easy. Do what's right.

# 42 | "Doing things well is more important than doing new things."

I love experiencing things that are new to me. Whether that's a food I've never tasted, a place I've never been, or an activity I've never tried, it's exhilarating to taste, touch, see, feel, and smell the unfamiliar. When you activate your senses, your mind gets a jolt of positive energy.

Having said that, I also believe that it's more important to develop strengths and skills than to spend your life bouncing around from one activity to another. You probably know the phrase, "jack of all trades, master of none". This applies to the person who is a chronic "dabbler". They jump in and out of activities and interests—even jobs and relationships. They dabble in one hobby and bounce to another without ever building proficiency. They try out a job or a learning program, but drop out before maximizing the potential. What's the point?

Let's say you decide to learn to play the violin and spend a few months taking lessons and then give up. You know the basics, but you certainly can't say you play the violin. What did you gain from the time you put into the experience? Did you give up because you didn't like the violin or did you get distracted by something else? And how long did this "something else" hold your interest?

Time is a precious commodity. You can spend it or invest it. When you spend time, you hand it over without expecting any "profit" in return— that's why they call it "killing time", because it's gone for good, with nothing to show for it. You can spend time watching television or playing video games. You can kill time at the mall, because you've got nothing better to do, but I have to wonder, do you *really* have no better way to use that time? Could you be helping someone, reading a book to expand your knowledge, taking a class online, improving your fitness, or improving your proficiency at something?

Conversely, investing your time is like investing your money. You do so with the expectation of gaining something in return. When you invest money, you expect to earn more money; otherwise, it's a wasted effort with nothing to show.

> **"** *...investing your time is like investing your money. You do so with the expectation of gaining something in return."*

Are you going to spend your time or invest it? If you want to invest your valuable time, what can you do to earn the greatest reward? Well, if you delve deeply into a subject, interest, hobby, activity, sport, or skill, and put your best effort into becoming really strong in this area, then you have added a skill dividend to your time investment portfolio. You can draw on this expertise throughout your life. That's the payback. Sure, some kids might argue that being a great gamer is a real skill, but unless that person is going to design or program video games for a living, what value does it add to the "time investment portfolio"? How will this skill help others? What knowledge value does it have in the long run?

Of course, young people are evolving, so they need to explore the world around them. It's important for them to dabble here and there, but it's never too soon to teach them the value of proficiency. I stuck with my piano lessons because I wanted to prove to my parents that I wouldn't give up. In the end, I gained a valuable skill that has stayed with me for a lifetime. Had I given up without achieving the level of accomplishment that I did, I would not have continued to play the piano and really enjoy the music I could make with this instrument.

If you spend your life continually moving on to a new skill or interest before you have become really good at something prior, you've tossed away the opportunity to not only enjoy the talent you acquired, but to pass it along to others. I have shared my love of music by teaching others. And I expect that a few of them inspired others to take up an instrument. If one person can inspire or teach three others, who each pass it along to three others, then 12 people have benefitted from the passion of one. And it will keep growing exponentially from there.

But you can't inspire or teach others until you've honed your skills. If you're not polished enough to rise above the crowd, people have nothing to gain from you.

A person who wants to teach in public school, for example, can do so with a bachelor's degree, at least in most states. If you want to teach at the college level, you need an advanced degree. It makes sense. You need to be more knowledgeable than the students you teach, so you invest in that proficiency.

Professionals in any industry are people who are paid for their particular knowledge, skill, or talent. An individual who is well-rounded, but not particularly strong in any area, doesn't offer unique value. However, if that person commits to being exceptional in a chosen area, he gathers more knowledge and fine-tunes his abilities so that he has more to offer than other people. That effort and achievement creates real value.

College students face a huge challenge as they try to discover that specialty. According to studies, on average, many college students change their majors three times before earning a degree; more than 50 percent switch at least once. With all this changing, students are more commonly taking five or six years to complete a four-year degree. It's tough to decide as a teenager what you want to do for the rest of your life, so I can understand why they need to change majors, and I applaud them for not just sticking with something that doesn't fit. But I think that if we do a better job helping young people invest their time instead of just spend it, we guide them toward a better, more focused future. Children can be so over-scheduled—running from one activity to another—that they become good, but not great. Parents try so hard to give their children diverse experiences that they don't afford them the opportunity to invest in becoming great. The result is a generation of well-rounded, but not particularly exceptional, young people. This pattern fosters mediocrity.

We need to help children slow down and take the time required to be exceptional. Let them be the best they can be—whether that's a chosen hobby, school subject, interest, activity, or sport. If we encourage them to avidly pursue an interest and then give them the time to do it—even if that means cutting out some of that "diversity"—we're ultimately helping them to discover the rewards of being great at something. Their self-esteem and confidence gets a big boost on occasions when someone tells them, "You're so good at that!"

# 43

## "Saying 'I tried' only means 'I failed', but with an excuse. In the end, it's still failure."

Back in the Garden of Eden, Adam took a bite of the forbidden fruit (or an apple, as many people know it) which God had warned him not to do. When He asked the first man why he ignored the warning, Adam basically said, "It's Eve's fault. She gave it to me."

When God asked Eve why she picked the forbidden fruit, she blamed Satan for tempting her to pluck the apple from the tree of knowledge of good and evil.

Thus was the original sin.

And the original excuses.

Certainly, Adam and Eve both *tried* not to succumb to the temptation. We don't know how hard they tried—maybe days, hours, or just minutes. In the end, they failed. It doesn't matter who was tempted by whom. They gave into the temptation, against God's warning.

When a person tries and fails, but uses an excuse, it doesn't change the outcome.

Here's an exchange I overheard once. It was a conversation between a father and teenaged son.

"How did you do on your math test?" Dad asked.

"Well, I accidentally failed," the boy answered.

"Accidentally?"

"Well, I didn't mean to fail. I tried really hard," he answered.

"Well," Dad responded, not masking his sarcasm, "as long as you didn't do it on purpose. I'd hate to think you tried to fail."

Does anyone try to fail? I don't think so. But they do *try* to find excuses for failures. We call this "The Blame Game", but in this game, there are no winners. The person looking for the one to blame is *failing* to accept responsibility for not achieving the desired result.

"Try" is a word that has a built-in exemption. "Try" gives you an out when you fail. Saying you will "try" shows hesitation and doubt. "I'll try to be there on time" implies that it's a possibility, but not a sure thing. "I'll try to get the sink fixed this weekend" offers no certainty that the leak will be repaired this weekend, or at all.

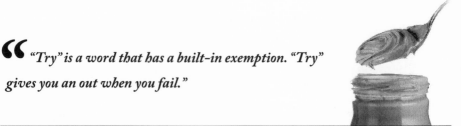

**❝** *"Try" is a word that has a built-in exemption. "Try" gives you an out when you fail."*

In other words, don't count on it. You've basically established a self-fulfilling prophecy, because you haven't committed wholeheartedly to doing your best.

Jiddu Krishnamurti said, "Don't say, 'I will try and do it'—that's one of the most evasive statements you can ever make. Either you do it, or you don't do it—there is no trying, or doing your best." (*Meeting Life: Writings and Talks on Finding Your Path Without Retreating from Society*, page 127).

"Try" is a non-committal word, like "maybe". They are both terms that connote indecision. When a child asks for something and mom or dad says, "Maybe", it leaves a flicker of hope in the child's mind. In truth, the response usually means "I'm going to say 'no', but I don't want to argue with you right now." The word "try" has the same impact as "maybe". You're not saying **will** achieve something, only that you'll give it a go. And when you decide to try, you tell yourself you don't have to put your best effort into whatever it is you're attempting. You've got an escape clause, so if things don't work out, you can say, "Well, I tried."

Fine. You tried, but you didn't do it, did you? How hard did you try? Did you honestly exhaust all effort and opportunity? Or did you just give up when things didn't fall into place as easily or quickly as you wanted?

To me, trying without success means something is left unfinished. You can come to me and say, "I tried, but I'm not done yet," and I'll give you an extension, offer help, or revise the plan. But if you come to me and shrug off the incomplete result with "Oh, well, at least I tried", then I'm going to see you as someone who doesn't care about results.

You shouldn't tackle a challenge with the thought that you are merely going to try, because you set yourself up for less than stellar results. And when you fail at the task but use the excuse that "I tried", you are refusing to accept responsibility for the outcome.

If you try and succeed, you will certainly bask in the glory. Well, if you are willing to take the credit, then you should be equally prepared to accept responsibility for the opposite result, without excuses or affixing blame elsewhere.

Ben Franklin was a man who tried and failed on many occasions, and then tried and succeeded. He invented the lightning rod, furnace stove, bifocals, long-arm (to grab items out of reach), swim fins (for the hands), odometer, and a flexible urinary catheter. He said, "He that is good for making excuses is seldom good for anything else."

The other consequence of using "I tried" as an excuse for failure or incompletion is that you begin to accept this as a valid measure. When you tell yourself often enough that you made an attempt, you will come to see even minor effort as acceptable. You continue to lower expectations. As a result, others will follow suit. Before long, the expectations are so low that you can trip over them.

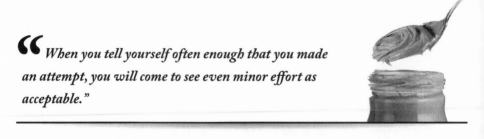

**❝** *When you tell yourself often enough that you made an attempt, you will come to see even minor effort as acceptable.* ❞

Is that the reputation you want—either for yourself or your child?

We need to teach young people that effort is important, but it's no substitute for results. I don't propose that we push our kids to over-achieve, but we do should instill in them that they need to be honest with themselves in this regard. In many, many cases, they must do more than try, because they will be measured on results, not attempts.

In track and field, for the field events—like the javelin, discus, long jump, shotput, and high jump—the athletes get three attempts. They are scored according to their best attempt. If it's not good enough, they don't place in the top three and earn no points. Saying, "But I really tried!" is not going to change the outcome.

In baseball, when a batter gets three strikes, he's out. You won't see a player say to his teammates, "Oh, well, I tried." A strikeout is still a strikeout.

Language is a powerful motivator. When you take on a challenge, you should approach it with the belief that "I will" and not "I will try." You'll work harder when you make this declaration out loud. "I **will** be there on time!" "I **will** fix the sink and I **will** do it this weekend!"

*" When you take on a challenge, you should approach it with the belief that "I will" and not "I will try.""*

Many things in life don't offer a second chance or a "do-over". So, you need to put forth your best effort the first time. Set a good example by creating more accountability in yourself.

Chuck Gallozzi, speaker, coach, and author of "The 3 Thieves and 4 Pillars of Happiness", wrote about planting a garden of success.[8]

*"First, plant 3 rows of peas:*

*Patience*

*Positive thinking*

*Persistence*

*Next, plant 3 rows of squash:*

*Squash excuses.*

*Squash blame.*

*Squash criticism.*

*Then, plant 3 rows of lettuce:*

*Let us be responsible.*

*Let us be trustworthy.*

*Let us be ambitious.*

[8] Gallozzi, Chuck, "Making Excuses", http://www.personal-development. com/chuck/excuses.htm

*Finish, with 3 rows of turnips:*

> *Turn up when needed.*

> *Turn up with a smile.*

> *Turn up with confidence."*

Since they will reap what they sow, help your children plant this garden. They'll harvest great success with it.

# 44 | "If you don't make your own decisions, someone else will make them for you."

Indecision *is* a decision. When you don't make a choice, you're actually making the decision not to decide. And what that says is that, if the decision is important enough, it will be made, with or without you.

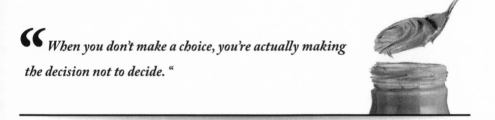

**❝** *When you don't make a choice, you're actually making the decision not to decide.* "

Indecision can result from procrastination—you just don't feel like you have to make a choice right now. It can wait. Well, that's a choice. You've decided to put off dealing with the issue right now. The consequence of waiting, therefore, is yours to bear. Maybe you put off doing your tax return until April 15. Then you realize you don't have the information you need to complete all the documents. The outcome of you *deciding* to wait is that you're going to either incur a late penalty or take a guess and perhaps enter the wrong information. So, the consequence might be a tax audit, because you decided not to do your taxes in a more timely manner.

Maybe you don't make a decision because you're not ready to commit to the responsibility of the choice. You're not sure you want to buy a house because of what you've seen in the housing market. Sure, the interest rates and housing prices are at an all-time low and it's really enticing, but you can't commit to such a big purchase. The cost of not making the decision at that time is that, when you *are* ready, you will likely pay more for your house, both purchase price and the mortgage interest. That's perfectly fine, as long as you accept that this is the cost for indecision.

Some people put off making a will. They know they **should** do it, but procrastinate. I know plenty of people who have ignored the need for estate and financial planning. They choose to put it off. Why? I think of my wife and my children. If anything were to happen to me, I don't want a judge to decide how my estate is going to be handled, nor do I want my family to have to wait until the probate court can come to a decision.

When you fail to make a decision, you set yourself up for loss. People who can't decide miss out on opportunities. Whether you're eyeing something on eBay and can't convince yourself that it's worth bidding on, or you can't commit to marriage, you're going to lose out. Someone else will end up with what you let get away—whether it's a hard-to-find collectible or an even harder-to-find soul mate.

**❝** *When you fail to make a decision, you set yourself up for loss. People who can't decide miss out on opportunities.* ❞

I have friends who have difficulty making even simple decisions. What movie do you want to see? Where should we go for dinner? What color are you going to paint that room? It's agony being with indecisive people when you're decisive, because you want to reach in and grab an answer from them. You're sitting in a restaurant, waiting for them to finalize their order so you can get your meal. Or you're with someone who has to try on the same outfit over and over and over again before deciding on whether or not to buy it.

Indecisive people are often afraid of making the wrong decision. So, rather than have to deal with the outcome of a wrong decision, they make none at all. Fear can be a paralyzing thing. No matter what scares you, it's holding you back, so confront the fear. If you suffer from "decidophobia", you're choosing to let your fear limit you.

I am more inclined to make a decision and not worry so much about whether it was a good or bad one. Hopefully, I'm right, but if not, I know I can take action to fix it. Making no decision is far worse, in my opinion, than making the wrong choice.

> **❝ *Making no decision is far worse, than making the wrong choice.* ❞**

I've discovered that people who avoid making minor decisions will avoid making major ones as well. They don't isolate their indecisiveness into just one corner of their world. While I admit that there are times when I truly don't care about the choice, I am perfectly comfortable in those situations with letting someone else decide. I consciously made my choice not to choose; I didn't just let the decision hang out there, waiting to be plucked.

I find it interesting that the root of the word "decide" comes from the Latin "decido", which means to "fall down" or "collapse". Deciduous means "falling off maturity", so deciduous trees and plants are those that drop their leaves or needles when they are past maturity. Making a decision is also referred to as "taking the plunge", which relates to this literal meaning (although the phrase more accurately refers to someone diving into deep water).

Indecisiveness doesn't have to be a chronic condition. There are ways to overcome the obstacles to making a decision. Try these with your child.

1. **Write down the pros and cons.** Letting everything bounce around in your head just clogs up the gears and prevents you from moving forward. When you put all the factors in writing, you can see your options more clearly. Include the consequences, too. "If I choose this, then this will happen."

2. **Put a value on your choices.** Rate the possibilities. If your child is trying to choose, for instance, whether to join one club or another, ask her how much each pro and con is worth, on a scale of 1 to 5. Is it more important to you to be with friends you have or with people who could become friends? Is it more important to learn something new or work on building a skill or interest you have? Add it up and use the total score the guide you.

3. **Give yourself a deadline.** We all need boundaries. Deadlines are a great way to get us to act. When we know the time a flight is leaving, we have to be there on time or miss the plane. When Christmas rolls around, your shopping days are over. When the timer goes off, you'd better get your dinner out of the oven or it's going to be ruined. Use the same deadline approach for making a decision. Write it on your calendar and stick with the deadline you've set.

4. **Don't take a survey.** The worst thing you can do when struggling with making a decision is to ask everyone around you for an opinion. First of all, the more opinions you get, the more confused you will be. And remember that they're not the ones who have to live with the consequence, so it's easy for them to choose for you.

5. **Take a deep breath and dive in.** As Nike tells us, "Just do it!" Stop procrastinating. Just close your eyes and choose. If you need to make changes, you can do it later, but at least, you're not just lingering on the diving board while everyone is watching you.

A leader is not afraid of making a decision. He accepts the responsibility. And he knows that there are lots of choices to be made, so by wasting time endlessly pondering the possibilities, he is delaying other decisions. That could be holding up people, action, and progress. I'm not proposing hasty decision-making, but it doesn't have to be a long, drawn-out process. Don't allow yourself or your child to be the proverbial cog in the wheel. Choose to choose.

# 45 | "Count your blessings, not your problems."

Load up your problems and put them on a mental scale. Then do the same with your blessings. Which weighs more? Why is it that the rough spots in your life take up so much more space in your mind than the good things? Far too often, we take our blessings for granted. Things like waking up every day, with a roof over your head, food in the fridge, and a little money in your pocket—those are more valuable than you might recognize. You're able to see, hear, smell, walk, and talk. Even if you're doing so with help from someone or something else, each of those abilities is a gift.

**❝** *You're able to see, hear, smell, walk, and talk. Even if you're doing so with help from someone or something else, each of those abilities is a gift."*

When something makes you smile, count that moment among your blessings. Even when you cry, your heart is beating. It's like the Tin Man said in the "Wizard of Oz" after finally receiving his greatest wish, a heart. "Now I know I have a heart, because it's breaking."

We get so wrapped up in what we don't have and things that go wrong that we fail to weigh in on what's going right. Bills are mounting up, the job isn't great, and certain people are just making life difficult. The bad stuff has a habit of snowballing. Something happens and you're at a loss to find the answer. Well, that's taking away your ability to deal with other issues that should have your attention. So, the troubles mount up and you feel like you're going to crumble under the weight of it.

You might turn to your God and ask for help to get you through this dark time. When the solution doesn't automatically appear, you might think your prayers weren't answered, but just maybe you prayed for the wrong thing. Or maybe you didn't see that God did, in fact, answer your prayer. He probably answered in such a way that was in your best interest and not necessarily in line with your immediate desires.

> **❝** *When the solution doesn't automatically appear, you might think your prayers weren't answered, but just maybe you prayed for the wrong thing."*

And timing.

I suggest you use some of this precious time to see those blessings. Every new day is a gift. It's a chance to reshape your life, or at least see it more clearly.

I don't subscribe to the popular idiom that "God doesn't give us anything we can't handle." During those times that try our patience, our strength, and our conviction, we might feel battered, we might look up to the heavens and plead, "Why?"

That's the wrong question. You'd be better served to ask, "What am I missing?"

Ask yourself right now, "What are the good things in my life that I am overlooking?" Think simply. Life, health, family, friends, and sustenance are the basic ones. Those are your foundation. Everything else is a bonus.

> **❝** *Think simply. Life, health, family, friends, and sustenance are the basic ones. Those are your foundation. Everything else is a bonus."*

While working on this book, I came across a blog post by Jen Lenks ("Life: As I See It") that beautifully illustrated "Count your blessings, not your problems." She wrote about her father's experience during chemotherapy:

"A relative 'newbie' on the oncology floor, he was in the midst of his fifth or sixth go-round with the toxic stuff when twin three- or four-year olds bound in the room with their thirty-something mother.

As she talked with the nurse, the two tow-heads called dibs on a seat on either side of my father. His reaction was typical of a sixty-five year old man facing treatment for a disease that he knew full well was going to eventually take him.

'I've got another two hours on the drip and, lucky me, I've got Frick and Frack along for a sideshow.' He could not believe how a mother could bring the kids along to watch her hooked up to an IV.

How insensitive—to all involved. Sick people should not have to deal with…this.

During our conversation, Dad questioned the 'stroke that babe must be married to'. He wondered what could be so goddamn important that the father could not take the kids while mom headed to the hospital.

As the nurse approached the boy next to him and another headed toward the girl on his other side, dad was enlightened.

Mom did not have cancer. The children did.

And on that particular day, he shared his wisdom with me. 'Be grateful you have two healthy kids. Cherish every cancer-free, pain-in-the-ass moment with them.'

He then revealed he spent the rest of the treatment counting his blessings. At least his diagnosis came during the 'winter' of his life...those poor kids were experiencing it at the beginning of their 'springtime'."[9]

When you stop dwelling in the negative, a whole world of opportunity opens up. It's like you swatted away all that dense fog that was clouding your perspective. Think positively and keep hope in your heart at all times. When you give up on that, what's left? You give yourself up to be buried alive in negative thinking. It's like a sinkhole. But you aren't swallowed up by the earth. When you ignore the good things in your life, you're diving into that sinkhole. Why would you do that when you have solid ground right beneath your feet?

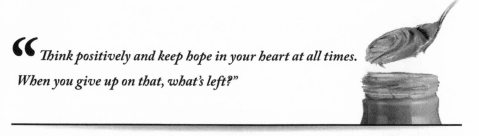

**❝** *Think positively and keep hope in your heart at all times. When you give up on that, what's left?"*

I often think about people who live simply. They live within their means, not trying to keep up with anyone or anything. They don't care about trends. They don't have big-screen televisions all over their house or take lavish vacations. They don't trade in their car every few years, but choose to invest in maintaining the one they have—not because they can't afford a new one, but don't feel the need for having one. They don't pay for a gym membership, but instead take long walks, bike rides, or jog. They kayak and hike. They work in their own gardens, even when they could pay to have someone handle the "chore". And you know what? They're happy. They appreciate what they have. Without all the physical and emotional clutter in their worlds, they can see the wonder of their blessings.

What challenges are you facing right now? How much does that all matter in the bigger picture of your entire life? Look beyond today and ask yourself,

9    JenLenks, "Count Your Blessings...Not Your Problems; http://www.chica-gonow.com/life-as-i-see-it/2011/08/count-your-blessings-not-your-problems

"Will this be important next month or next year?"

Don't wait till Thanksgiving to count your blessings. Like Valentine's Day, anniversaries, birthdays, Mother's Day, and Father's Day, a holiday shouldn't have to remind you to appreciate the special people in your life. We don't need to wait till Veterans Day to thank a soldier for serving our country. And it shouldn't take a tragedy like Sandy Hook or 9/11 to make you hug your family and tell them you love them.

Teach your children to appreciate what they have. When they complain about something that has gone wrong, ask them to share two blessings. Then ask which one weighs more. Give them the gift of valuing the life they have, not the things they covet. In the end, you'll raise a child who will feel fulfilled without the trappings of our culture and will be able to serve those people who need help.

**❝ *When they complain about something that has gone wrong, ask them to share two blessings. Then ask which one weighs more.*❞**

Count your blessings together, because they add up to a more joy-filled life.

# 46

## "Your life is not a rehearsal."

Youth is a time for making mistakes. Kids experiment with possibilities. They try things that might not work out the way they expected. With a lot of prayer and guidance, they learn from mistakes and become wiser. Trial and error is important in the growing process. You learn not to touch a hot iron, that a painful sunburn could have been prevented, and that not everyone is your friend. These are lessons that will serve you well in the future, because the knowledge gained will help you avoid similar mistakes.

Well, it *should*.

When you're young, you feel invincible. We all did things "back then" that we would never do now. We are wiser or, at the very least, more experienced. We know that we are mortal.

As adults, we know things—like it's better never to start smoking, because it's hard to stop. We know that teen pregnancy can happen to anyone, including the straight A student, the star athlete, and the kid from a "nice family". We also know that texting while driving is a deadly choice.

Looking back, we can see that a lot of things we were forced to learn in school had merit, even though it seemed so lame at the time. As much as you hated learning fractions and percentages, you use that knowledge every day. The teacher who was a stickler for spelling and grammar was a major pain when you were sweating through that class, but your writing improved as a result. And you learned so many lessons that still stick in your mind today—"i" before "e" except after "c", when to use "me" instead of "I", and how to spell "surprise", "occasion", and "Mississippi".

Every choice you make in life is like adding a stone to a rock wall. Make the right decision and you strengthen the wall. Choose poorly and it can all come tumbling down. Sure, not every decision has monumental consequences, but I, at least, like to know what those outcomes could be.

**"** *Every choice you make in life is like adding a stone to a rock wall. Make the right decision and you strengthen the wall. Choose poorly and it can all come tumbling down."*

Life is **not** a rehearsal. You're not practicing for the live performance where it's okay to mess up because you'll get it right "when it counts". You can't go back and do it again and fix what went wrong. You can apologize but there's no "Erase" button on your life. So, important choices should be made carefully,

**"** *You can't go back and do it again and fix what went wrong. You can apologize but there's no "Erase" button on your life."*

Look at the divorce rate in the United States. Almost half of marriages end in divorce. Of those people who give marriage another try, about 60 percent will get divorced again. Young people have grown up in a culture where breakups are common—actually, the norm. Among their parents, their friend's parents, and their relatives, divorce will likely occur. In addition, they see celebrities go in and out of marriages like a revolving door. So, they are not accustomed to perceiving the decision to get married as a deep, lasting commitment. It's a promise that's easily broken. If it doesn't work out, there's always divorce, right?

But we shouldn't be entering into relationships—with a significant other or employer—with the mindset of "we'll see how it goes." That direction leads to doing less than you can or should. Having a relatively "easy out" is the safety net that enables people to make choices without considering the consequences, but it's those consequences that punctuate your life. You carry them with you—a former employee, ex-husband/wife, ex-girlfriend/boyfriend, recovering addict, or dropout. You can move on and change your life for the better after surviving life's downturns, but isn't it just better to treat your life as a live performance rather than a rehearsal?

**"** *Having a relatively "easy out" is the safety net that enables people to make choices without considering the consequences, but it's those consequences that punctuate your life."*

# 47 | "Finish."

Every person's actions, decisions, relationships, and experiences create a portfolio of their life thus far. If you flip through the pages of an individual's book, you'll get a pretty good picture of who they are—active or passive, driven or indifferent, dedicated or just showing up.

The older we get, the more detailed a profile this portfolio presents. For example, if you've been fairly successful along the way—all the way back to earning accolades in school, sports, and activities as a child—then you probably will continue the pattern. If you've carried a defeatist attitude or been unwilling to accept responsibility for your decisions, then your portfolio will be defined by these habits and traits. You can change your job, your home, your spouse, and your environment, but if your mindset remains the same, then your future will continue to reflect your past.

You are not what you eat, but what you've done—and *not* done. Some people leave a trail of unfinished plans, ideas, and acts in their wake. They start plenty, but then walk away before the job is done and move on to some other endeavor. Why? Maybe it was too complex, too time-consuming, or just didn't generate the immediate results they wanted, or at least, didn't deliver fast enough for their taste. They don't want to put the effort into maintaining relationships, so they leave them. For whatever reason, these people live unfinished lives.

The worst thing you can do is to embark on a task without thinking ahead about what it will require to finish—and then quitting. Giving up can easily become a bad habit. Maybe a child doesn't excel at baseball or gymnastics and then gives up on the sport. The youth tries another sport and has equally lackluster results. He quits again. Quite possibly, he gives up on athletics altogether, just based on a couple of experiences. But look at Michael Jordan. He was cut from his high school basketball team because he wasn't good enough. Imagine if one of the all-time best basketball players had given up on the sport as a teenager!

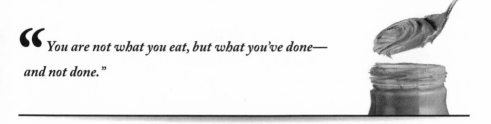

**❝** *You are not what you eat, but what you've done— and not done.* **"**

Maybe a child joins a club and then decides it takes too much time or isn't all that fun, so he quits. He takes up an instrument and joins the school band, but his friends aren't in it, so he bows out. Now look at Kalia Cove as an example. She could have used her health as an excuse to get out of Girl Scout cookie sales. The 11 year-old had three heart surgeries before she was even two years old. She couldn't attend public school because of the threat of germs, which could kill her. But she put on a protective mask and invested hours upon hours in selling Girl Scout cookies—and sold 3,503 boxes in 2011, the most of any Girl Scout in western Washington state. When you think about Kalia's achievement, the excuse of "I don't feel like it" just doesn't cut it, does it?

Now let's fast forward a few years with the other youngster I've been describing. He makes plans with his friends, but often changes his mind and cancels on them. In college, he has some tough classes, so he drops them. Giving up has become a pattern.

Compare this behavior to Steven Spielberg. He applied twice for admission to the film school at the University of Southern California and was rejected both times. If he took those rejections to heart, we would never have had movie classics, like "E.T.", "Schindler's List", "Jaws", and "Saving Private Ryan", and the Indiana Jones trilogy.

As this other young person continues along the path of an unfinished life, he finds himself with a boss or a job that isn't exactly ideal, so he quits. He tries hobby after hobby, investing money each time in his newfound passion, but the excitement wanes and he moves on to something else.

Somewhere along the line, this type of person hasn't connected the dots between expectations and reality. He underestimates any number of factors—time, effort, energy, cost, and gratification. And because he learned from an early age that quitting is an easy way out, he falls back on this pattern. Meanwhile, he leaves behind a wake of incompleteness—a trail that will dog him if he doesn't commit to following through and achieving goals. Success does not come from starts and stops. Leaders don't inspire others by giving up easily. They demonstrate perseverance and commitment.

**"** *Success does not come from starts and stops. Leaders don't inspire others by giving up easily. They demonstrate perseverance and commitment."*

I made a mistake early in my career that I regret to this day. Right after graduating from college, I was trying to find a job. I contacted a family member who was well connected in the business community. I asked for his help in finding a job and he told me to go see a friend of his who would give me some assistance. He contacted the person and let him know who I was and why I would be getting in touch. This person made a special effort on my behalf because he believed in me and wanted to help me get ahead.

Well, I didn't follow through. I don't quite know why. I just didn't contact him. And the more time that passed, the harder it seemed to make that call, because I was embarrassed that I had dropped the ball. By not calling him, not only did I communicate disinterest, but I also demonstrated to a family member that I didn't value his time or interest. Neither was true, of course, but I sure didn't present myself as I should have.

There were some things that I was striving to achieve back then. Had I been more persistent, the outcomes could have made a significant impact on my life, but I'll never know because they were abandoned—left unattended and incomplete. Even though I've been relatively successful in my life in spite of this blunder, I wonder how some of my decisions—and indecisions—might have changed my life.

Many years later, there were times when I could have benefitted from this family member's contact, but I knew I couldn't go to him because I made a bad impression right from the start. Since I didn't take advantage of this wonderful opportunity when it was handed to me, it was gone for good. Opportunities are never lost. They are embraced by others.

**"** *Opportunities are never lost. They are embraced by others."*

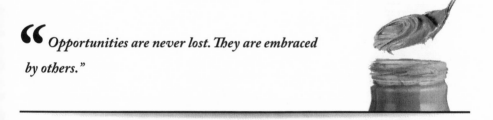

Regret is never good. Living with "What Ifs" in your life leaves you guessing about what might have been. Unfortunately, you will never know.

When you're mentoring children, it's important to impress upon them the importance of finishing what you start. Quitting is an option that should be used only when all else fails. It's a bad habit that will hinder a person from achieving their potential. Just share these examples with them:

- J.K. Rowling's first "Harry Potter" manuscript was rejected by 12 publishers.

- John Grisham's first book, "A Time to Kill", was rejected by 16 literary agents, but once accepted and published, it sold more than 250 million copies.

- Dr. Seuss—Theodor Geisel—had to push his way through 27 rejections before his first book was accepted.

- Abraham Lincoln ran for a variety of offices and failed 12 times to be elected.

- Beethoven's music teacher told him he was hopeless as a composer.

- It took Thomas Edison more than 10,000 attempts before he successfully invented the light bulb. When asked why he didn't give up after all those failures, he said, "I haven't failed 10,000 times. I've simply succeeded in finding 10,000 ways that definitely won't work."

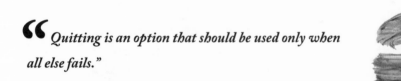

*Quitting is an option that should be used only when all else fails."*

It's hard to build commitment and tenacity in young people. They get frustrated when things don't come easy. We need to remind them that they won't enjoy an activity until they master it, and they can't master it without effort.

We may believe we can achieve something and have it pegged for "someday" in our list of dreams, but that vision has no value in the real world. You will be measured by your achievements, not by what you think you can do or what you hope to do someday. Intentions have no value in the world. Results do.

*Intentions have no value in the world. Results do."*

Henry Wadsworth Longfellow said, "We judge ourselves by what we feel capable of doing, while others judge us by what we have already done."

I mentioned earlier about learning the piano, but let me fill in some important details here. When I was a child, I admit I had a habit of setting a goal and then dropping it. I had taken up the trumpet and the tuba, but lost interest. When I was 13, I told my parents that I wanted to learn to play the piano. They didn't share my enthusiasm because they had already witnessed how quickly my commitment dwindled with other endeavors. They told me, "Fine, but you have to figure out how to get to your lessons and we're not buying you a piano, so you have to find a way to practice."

Their belief that I would give up was like a match that ignited a challenge in me. I would prove them wrong! I rode my bike to my piano teacher's house. Mrs. Bessie Smith, a family friend who lived up the street, had a piano and allowed me to practice there. I also used the piano at a local church. Whenever I felt like I didn't want to practice, I reminded myself that my parents had become so accustomed to me quitting that they didn't believe I could stick with anything. I was the boy who cried wolf! I needed to prove something to them but, even more importantly, to myself.

I earned an even greater reward from those efforts than learning to play the piano. I went on to write, orchestrate, and conduct music. Later, because of my ability to identify and write on trends in the music industry, I was asked to become the music editor of an industry magazine where I met a record company executive-- I eventually married her. Had I not been persistent in proving my parents wrong about pursuing the piano, I might never have met this amazing woman!

Coming up against a challenge is not a reason to back away. Anything worth having requires effort. If it were easy, everyone would have or do it. When a child is teetering on quitting, ask her to list the reasons for her choice. Discuss consequences and alternatives. Talk about what that choice says about her.

**"** *Coming up against a challenge is not a reason to back away. Anything worth having requires effort."*

Stick it out. You don't get to the good stuff without effort!

Life is too precious to leave it undone. Finish—and do it with gusto!

# Please come back!

I hope the ideas in this book have sparked some thought about the way you mentor a child, or for that matter, anyone who desire to become a better leader. But please understand that even though you may have come to the end of this list of Peanut Butter Principles, you have not reached the end. We all continue to grow and learn from our experiences. We need to remember to share them, to pass along even those lessons that may seem small to us, because they may be huge for someone else. They might stick like peanut butter!

I also suggest that you take the time to ensure your child understands the meaning of these principles. Let them ask questions and encourage them to give you an example from their own life to illustrate the concept. When they truly understand an idea, they will be able to apply it.

It's my hope that you will work through each life lesson, one at a time, with a youngster. Read it together, talk about it, and put it in a context that the child can relate to. And revisit these thoughts on a regular basis. You can make it a weekly family activity or integrate the lessons into a class curriculum. However, whenever, and wherever you can, please give the children in your world the chance to benefit from the experience of others.

Finally, this list of 47 Peanut Butter Principles may keep growing. I hope it will, because that means that, as I stated earlier in this book, I am still growing and learning, that I am gaining a valuable return on the investment of my time. And you can be sure that when I have amassed more sticky thoughts, I will share them with you.

Thank you!

—Eric Franklin

# ABOUT THE AUTHOR

Eric Franklin has a passion for empowering people to maximize their abilities and opportunities. He has started several successful companies in information technology, music and entertainment, management consulting, healthcare, and dining. He is sought out for his expertise as a business coach and speaker through his "Getting Past Go" lecture series and is Chairman of the Southern Maryland Workforce Investment Board.

He lives in Maryland with his wife, Rané, and three children.

You can contact Eric Franklin at www.peanutbutterprinciples.com

Made in the USA
Charleston, SC
24 November 2013